Trucking Business Guide for Beginners

Start Your Owner-Operator Company With Less Headache

Shaun M. Durrant

Table of Contents

Introduction

"Starting your own business isn't just a job, it's a way of life." -Richard Branson

There are many business options out there for you to get into. However, as everyone knows, it's best to enter a business in which you already have some expertise. If you're a truck driver or have been driving in some capacity for a while, entering the world of a truck owner-operator makes perfect sense.

The fact is that truck owner-operators have the best of all worlds. Yes, the work is hard but this doesn't mean it's tough. While there is a learning curve, the challenges ahead of you aren't that different from what other business owners face. Many truckers allow the perceived challenges of running a business stop them from exploring this world, and it's a shame.

Anyone can start their own trucking business and you don't need any special qualifications to begin. You most certainly do not need any fancy degrees that add a bunch of letters to your name! Running a trucking business is all about fostering relationships and satisfying your clients' needs. This is something you've already been doing, whether you know it or not.

Having said that, there are nuances to the business that you need to learn about. Much like how you once learned to drive a truck, you need to learn the mechanics of the business to set yourself up for success in the long run. Many owner-operators jump into the business without preparing themselves for what lies ahead and end up losing everything.

By following the advice contained within these pages, you'll manage to not only have your own business up and running in no time, but also learn how to build processes that will sustain it over the long term, which is where most owner-operators struggle.

Starting a new business is relatively simple, but it is the day-to-day operations that can be very tricky. In this book, you will learn what it takes to become an owner-operator and how to ensure your success.

There is a common misconception that you require something special to become an owner-operator. This isn't true at all. What you need is good information that is backed by years of experience from someone who has been there and done that.

That is exactly what I'm offering you in this book.

Trucker to Owner-Operator

Trucking as an activity has always held a certain allure. It's one of those few jobs that offers the freedom of the road along with a good degree of independence. Truckers tend to be highly independent and opinionated people. Perhaps the very idea of sitting in an office is enough to send you running for the hills! I know that's how I react to the thought.

Running a business is simply the next step in your journey. One of the biggest advantages to this field is the ability to choose your hours and work for yourself. This won't be the case when you first start out, as you will need to put in your time, get some strong experience under your belt and work some long hours.

There are no shortcuts in this process. This is why the quicker you get started, the faster you'll get there! There is literally no reason for you to continue sitting on the sidelines, wondering whether you have what it takes. It's true that experienced truckers stand a better chance of running a successful business. However, the difference in their chances and the odds that a relatively inexperienced trucker faces are far lower than you may think. Everyone has to put in roughly the same amount of work at the end of the day. New truckers will have to work harder at certain aspects of the business.

To begin, it is important for you to prepare financially for this shift from a steady job to owning a business. This is something that many people underestimate, as it will change the way you view money and the value you provide.

With a typical job, you can rely on a steady stream of income at the end of the month. With owning your own business, you can't always rely on a steady stream of income. There will be a variation in your income and you will need to plan for this. In the first few months, you might not make any money. Ideally, you'll be prepared for this potential and can mitigate the situation.

Many new business owners jump in wearing rose-tinted glasses and neglect to consider the difficulties they may face. Being confident in your abilities is one thing. But it's important that you anticipate things will be tough for the first while and that you need to expect that you will be tested. This is a slightly negative outlook but it will prepare you for the journey ahead.

Ironically, you'll find yourself dealing with challenges as they come since they won't be unexpected for you.

The business side of trucking is a world you won't have been exposed to if you're currently driving. Typically, this is a world that new owner-operators underestimate. Many believe that it will be easy to find new clients and negotiate rates. I'm not saying it's difficult. However, there are many nuances you must be aware of before taking the plunge.

All of the information you will learn in this book are a product of my experiences in this industry. I began as an employee and I ventured into starting my own trucking business. I found that I was well-prepared in some areas but grossly underestimated others.

My Journey

My reasons for becoming an owner-operator were simple. I spent many hours on the road, away from my family, and at some point, I began to question whether it was all worth it. Sure, the paycheck was good but as you probably know, money isn't everything. Time is even more valuable and is something you can never get back.

I loved the idea of driving my rig and being my own boss but I had to be careful in making the transition. Financial concerns were at the top of my mind and I couldn't simply jump into being an owner-operator. This is what prompted me to conduct deep research into the ins and outs of being an owner-operator.

I had so many questions - many of which are likely the same as you have. How do you choose the right equipment? How do you ensure repeat clients? What's the real deal with load boards? I was fortunate to have a strong network of experienced owner-operators to help me, but truth be told, most of my learning was done the hard way.

This is to say I made mistakes and learned my lessons in the real world. There was no reason for my journey to be as tough as it was. My mission with this book is to help you avoid the pitfalls I experienced because of ignorance and a lack of vision. I'm not guaranteeing you won't face any issues. However, I want to help you avoid the mistakes I made.

Would I change any of it? Absolutely not! I've been an owner-operator for five years and have loved every minute of it! I love being out on the open road as much as I love coming back home to my family. I enjoy ironing out details with my loads and dealing with the wonderful people I have the privilege of working with.

Yes, I have bad days, just like anyone else. However, they pale in comparison to the good ones. My aim is to help you achieve this dream, as well. By picking up this book, you've displayed a willingness to educate yourself. Believe it or not, most people never even make it this far.

Now, it's time to move forward and take the next step! Reading this book isn't enough. You need to put everything into practice and start executing the tasks within. You will be afraid or nervous. Don't worry, this is perfectly normal. I assure you that you already have everything you need to be successful.

Without further ado, let's jump in and see whether you ought to become an owner-operator!

Chapter 1:

Should You Become an Owner-

Operator?

One of the most important questions to ask yourself before jumping into a business is whether you're well-suited to it. Running a business requires a shift in your mindset. You have less certainties to work with and will need to become comfortable with being uncomfortable.

This might sound crazy to you but it describes every successful owner-operator I know. Don't worry though. Adopting this mindset is a skill just like driving a big rig is. You can learn everything you need to be successful. This chapter is going to first walk you through the basics of the trucking industry, before examining the question of whether you ought to run a business or stick to being an employee.

Contrary to popular perception, I'm not here to demonize being an employee. Believe it or not, I think it's the right choice for many people. Running a business requires certain skills beyond driving that some people find distasteful. I'm not talking about ethics. I'm merely pointing out that all of us have strengths and some of us might not be predisposed to executing the tasks that a business demands.

So now that we've got that out of the way, let's jump in and examine this wonderful industry all of us work in!

The Trucking Industry

The best place to begin when talking about the trucking industry is with the numbers. In 2019, the market for freight movement was worth $791.7 billion USD. Trucking is roughly 70% of this market, as the majority of freight moved in the United States is via trucks. There isn't any sector that is untouched by trucking.

Everything from infrastructure, utilities, agriculture, wholesale manufacturing, retail outlets, chemicals, and even nuclear waste, relies on the trucking industry to execute their tasks. The United States is a huge country and for some reason, freight transport via rail has never fully developed.

While large shipments are transported via rail, it's far more economical to transport smaller shipments by road. Given the excellent interstate network, it's a given that the trucking industry is vital to our nation's economy. In many ways, trucks are the unsung heroes of business.

The trucking industry is often seen as invisible. When you think of the food you buy at a grocery store, you probably think of the farms that produce the food and the quality that the store maintains the goods in. You rarely think of the kind of truck that transported produce from the farm to the market. You probably don't spend much time wondering what sort of technology the truck had to ensure the fruit you're buying arrived in top quality.

The trucking industry is a subset of the larger supply chain sector. Officially, trucks fall under the logistics and transportation sector. You'll hear a number of terms being used interchangeably when referring to the business. You'll hear of logistics providers, 3PLs (third party logistics companies), shippers, carriers, and so on. Almost all of them rely on trucks, so don't let the fancy lingo throw you off.

If you're an experienced trucker, you've probably realized that the industry is cyclical. These cycles move in line with the economy and it's ironic that the business itself has an air of fragility about it. I'm not saying it's a bad business to enter into. It's just that there's a fine line between being wildly successful and failing at it. It's what leads many prospective owner-operators to stay away from setting up their own shop.

It was a misconception that I, too, carried for the longest time. However, I can assure you that running a successful owner-operator business is more about defining processes than luck. Yes, some luck is involved but its contribution is a lot less than you might imagine. Don't let the prospect of tough business conditions throw you off. Every industry is cyclical in nature and it's just something you'll become used to.

Trucking is a domestic business in America. The volume of overland transport is large enough to ensure that demand always exceeds supply. This makes trucks and truckers a valuable commodity. The bulk of the industry is controlled by large trucking companies that own their trucks and hire drivers as their employees or lease them out to drivers.

The lack of foreign currency involvement means that there is little risk of exchange rates eroding profits. This is both a good and bad thing. For one, it ensures that global economic events tend to have little impact on the trucking industry. The negative aspect is that you're intertwined with domestic events and can't rely on diverse economies to mitigate your risk. If you're a trucker, you're "all in" on America, whether you like it or not.

Personally, I like knowing that I can keep track of and understand the forces that affect my business. I don't have to worry about a foreign government official dictating terms that might end up negatively affecting my prospects. This is often the case in other industries. Trucking is a huge exception and you'll find that most truckers are highly empowered folks who make real contributions to our economy.

Being a trucker is a point of pride and owning your rig *is* a big deal. The logistics industry is vast and there is always demand for all kinds of truckers. These days, automation is increasing and it's undeniably a force to reckon with. The world is moving toward self-driving cars and a few companies have now begun trialing self-driving rigs.

I would be lying if I said this wasn't a threat to human owner-operators. I cannot predict what the industry will look like in 30 years time, but I can confidently say that self-driving technology isn't close to overtaking human driving in the next decade or two. It takes skill to operate a big rig and machines don't yet have the ability to replicate human skills.

So don't worry about the news that automation is taking jobs. I suppose this will eventually happen but as with all change, the industry will evolve to accommodate everyone. Bigger companies might switch to automated fleets but who is to say that you couldn't own one yourself? You could be an owner-operator with an automated truck, after all.

As it currently stands, this kind of talk is moot. There is a huge demand for skilled truckers and this only makes owner-operators valuable.

Types of Trucking Businesses

There are a number of different types of trucking businesses currently in the United States. Some of the following categories overlap with one another but they'll give you an idea of the variety of services that are offered. If you've been operating one kind of truck, consider switching categories if it appeals to you.

One of the most common services is the *door-to-door trucking service*. This is a consumer-oriented business where the trucker picks up goods from the manufacturer's doorstep and transports it directly to the consumer. Generally speaking, truckers require access to a logistics hub where packages can be sorted, since manufacturers will never ship in smaller loads. This is why you'll find that most door-to-door truckers work for a larger company or lease their trucks from them. The work is usually steady but it's seasonal. You'll find that volumes pick up during the holidays and there will be more than enough work to go around during those times.

Similar to door to door trucking is *B2B or business to business trucking*. The loads in this category are typically larger, and ironically, it's easier for an owner-operator to work within this sector. This is because shipments are usually received in bulk and another business typically receives them instead of a single consumer. The flipside is that this industry runs on networking and it might be tough for an unknown operator to break in. However, if you put in the legwork, you'll find that your network will bring you loads and you'll have no trouble accessing payment and negotiating terms.

Some examples of B2B goods that truckers ship are furniture, electronics, industrial parts and supplies, and other manufactured goods. Note that in some cases, your rig will need to be outfitted with special technologies to ensure the goods arrive safely. For instance, food transport is a B2B business but you'll need cold chain tech on your truck to ensure food remains safe.

The next category of truckers transport *heavy loads*. Technically all loads are heavy but when talking about d heavy loads or heavy hauls, these loads cannot be transported in conventional trucks. Typically, truckers seeking these jobs install special equipment for one-off loads. Every job in this category tends to be a custom one and a lot depends on the client in question.

Typically, government offices contract heavy hauls and the negotiation periods can be long. Since so much depends on the individual situation, there's no telling what rates are like. A lot also depends on how far the trucker will need to move the load. Still, rates are generally higher than the average market rate and it is a very lucrative niche to operate in.

Food deliveries are a category unto themselves, despite being largely B2B. This is because all food deliveries need a cold chain system to remain in a consumable state. These shipments are riskier from a trucker's perspective but they tend to pay well. These shipments can be B2B or B2C, despite the former being the majority. B2C shipments tend to incorporate last-mile deliveries, which can be risky.

Often, last-mile routes are unpredictable and even the slightest delay can compromise shipments. This leads to losses and truckers can't afford them. However, B2C tends to see greater shipment frequencies, even if loads are smaller. So there's a trade-off there. B2C cold chain equipment also tends to be smaller. You'll be driving an oversized ice cream truck or van in most cases, so it's not as if you'll need to fit a huge rig with cold chain tech, which could lead to more failures.

There are other ways to categorize trucking companies besides the loads they carry. Often, the nature of their loads and the source of business define categories. For instance, you'll hear a lot about for hire truckload carriers. These companies earn money by hauling freight for other companies.

They tend to have large fleets and appear very large on the outside. However, they are in the business of being a middleman. They own large fleets and lease them to large manufacturers for use. In many cases, they then turn around and charge their drivers a fixed monthly amount to lease the trucks. They connect manufacturers to truckers and collect what is effectively a commission for sitting in-between.

Some of these companies hire the truckers that they lease trucks to. However, the market these days is changing. Freight demand is cyclical and it's less risky for these companies to maintain contractors instead of employees. They often have multiple clients on their roster to spread the risk of freight turnover. If you're a new driver, or don't have significant experience in the industry, this might be a good place to begin. Just note that you won't own your truck or be a full-fledged owner-operator.

In contrast to for-hire truckload carriers, private fleet operators own both the manufacturing and transportation aspects of their business. For instance, Frito-Lay is a private fleet operator. They own their trucks and employ the drivers who transport their goods. Working for these companies is essentially being an employee. You're guaranteed monthly income, however you're also putting all of your eggs in one basket.

If the company suffers a downturn, you might find yourself out of a job. Sometimes, these companies offload work to owner-operators but these instances are rare.

The final category of truckers you'll find are LTL or less than truckload drivers. These can be owner-operators or large companies. LTL companies are an important part of the industry, despite there being a misconception that they're somehow operating an inefficient business model. The need for LTL truckers remains strong because many goods are too large to be shipped through regular channels but have too small a quantity to be shipped through a single trucker.

An LTL trucker ships these goods along with other freight to ensure a full truckload for themselves. They then deliver these goods to the necessary addresses. There are two categories of LTL truckers. The first are line truckers who shuttle goods from customers to freight distribution centers. The second are last mile truckers who deliver goods to consumers.

Aside from these categories, a special mention must be made of hazardous goods transporters. These truckers transport chemicals and nuclear waste. As such, it's a specialized category of transport and requires a great deal of special equipment to make it work. You'll have to invest a significant sum of money to make sure your rig complies with government regulations.

The positive side is that the work is steady and it's a relatively small industry. Once you break in, you're almost always guaranteed work and can be a "big fish in a small pond", so to speak. However, if you don't have connections in this sector and aren't experienced, it might be a good idea to strengthen your foundation before entering as an owner-operator.

Challenges of a Trucking Business

No business is without challenges and trucking is no different. In this section, I'm going to give you a realistic view of what it takes to be a successful trucking owner-operator. Some of my points might seem pessimistic but remember that I'm presenting a realistic picture of everything. My aim is to inform you of the realities so that you're under no illusions when you begin your business.

Drastic Initial Change

Initially, switching from being an employee to a business owner is challenging. As a trucker working for a company, you don't have much to deal with (believe it or not). Your rig is taken care of by the company and you don't need to worry about anything other than driving.

Most people enter the world of trucking because of their desire to hit the open road with a steady job. However, being a business owner is a different proposition. Your rig is now your own and you need to take care of it fully. Anything that goes wrong on it is your responsibility, as is your load. Where previously your company would take care of paperwork related to any issues affecting loads, you're the one who is now fully responsible and legally liable.

This jump can be too much for some drivers as they struggle to comprehend the challenge of being responsible for everything. However, if you enter the business with your eyes open and acknowledge that you have a responsibility to your clients, you'll find them easy to deal with.

Perhaps the biggest change occurs on the financial side of the business. You'll be responsible for maintaining your cash flow and can't rely on a steady stream of cash without putting in work. Don't forget, you still need to drive in between all of this. The tasks you'll need to execute will seem daunting. This is why it's essential for you to educate yourself before jumping in.

Patience

It seems odd to put patience on here, but please bear with me. As an employee, you're getting paid no matter what you do. As long as you deliver your goods on schedule, you're not going to face penalties or anything else. The customer or receiver can take as long as they want unloading goods and you're still getting paid.

However, new owner-operators are often surprised at how time conscious they become. You're getting paid to deliver goods, not to wait while they're being unloaded. This is often a problem with large consignments since it might take the receiver three or four hours to unload everything.

Meanwhile, you need to wait there, idling, without getting paid. You'll have to stagger your jobs appropriately and account for idling time when quoting rates. Often, these provisions might price you out of a job and you'll see it awarded to a trucker who doesn't know what they're doing. This will lead to frustration, but it's a reality in this business.

Margins are often thin and shippers are looking for the lowest rates. Balancing their needs with yours is a tough act and it might lead you to forego some contracts. New owner-operators often find this aspect of the business tough to deal with. The key is patience. Know that the right jobs will come your way as long as you remain focused and dedicated the rewards are worth it.

Lack of Parking

Have you ever driven a car around a busy city block looking for parking space? Well, imagine doing that in a big rig knowing you're on the clock and that a delay can mean a penalty. Even worse, if you park your rig in the wrong place, it might get stolen or vandalized and there goes your golden goose!

Parking is a bigger problem than most drivers realize. When driving a company rig, it's easy to drop it off at the designated location and then be on your way. You may encounter the odd problem on the road but these are easily handled as you're not stationary for that long.

The challenges of owning your rig make parking a complicated issue. Suddenly, it isn't some company rig that you are in charge of. You're essentially driving your financial future around, which brings its own challenges. Spaces that were once adequate will no longer do as you worry about security.

There's no easy way around this. You're driving a monster of a vehicle and parking is going to be an issue. While the challenge will remain, it will get easier to deal with as time goes on.

Safety

Aside from the possibility of your rig being vandalized while resting, there's also the question of on-road conditions. owner-operators earn money when the wheels turn. This leads newer

. rs to book as many loads as possible without
ınsidering their safety.

While Federal regulations mandate rest and drive hours, some
drivers play fast and loose with them and risk their health and
safety in the name of making more money. This often happens
to owners who experience the feast or famine syndrome where
they are either overloaded with jobs, or have none. When the
times are good, they overwork themselves and jeopardize
safety.

Working to steadily market yourself and spread the word about
your services is the way forward. This brings a steady stream of
potential jobs your way and you can rely on some semblance of
steady cash flow. It will be challenging at first but remember
that you should never jeopardize your health in the name of
earning additional money.

If you feel that you might be in a position to have to do this,
you might not have planned your business properly. Before
getting into the owner-operator game, you need enough of a
cash buffer to account for revenue shortfalls so that you don't
feel the need to always keep driving.

Freight Rate Fluctuations

Shipping is a seasonal business and the margins are thin.
Compounding the issue is the fact that everyone is looking to
beat one another in a race to the bottom. This makes being an
owner-operator tortuous at times since you'll see people
quoting rates that you know are impossible to earn a profit on.

Whatever you feel about this, it is a sad reality of the business
that there is no way around.In peak seasons, you'll face more
competition and may have to discount your rates and rely on

volumes. In lean seasons, you'll have to rely on your network to score jobs that pay well.

It's a balancing act at all times. Make no mistake: you're running a business and have to stay on top of everything. Cash flow fluctuations are challenging and they're the first major surprise that new owner-operators receive. How can you plan your spending and budgets when you don't know how much money you're going to receive at the end of the month?

This is why having a cash buffer at all times and planning your marketing activities in advance is so useful. Being a business owner is great but it also brings responsibilities that you have to shoulder. Live below your means and you'll never have to worry about a fluctuating cash flow. Create processes that bring customers to you and you won't worry about freight rate fluctuations.

There is a bigger picture to all this. The drive for automation is placing a negative pressure on shipping rates and owner-operators are feeling the pinch. It's led to an odd situation in the industry where there's a shortage of skilled drivers but rates remain low. A lot of this has to do with business conditions that are outside of your control.

However, this isn't a reason to be pessimistic. As I explained earlier, automation is still a long way from overtaking trucking jobs. Instead, it's important to develop a solid marketing plan that will account for both lean and strong periods of business. Consistency in marketing is what brings results. Yes, driving is a part of the job. However, as a business owner, you need to prioritize your time well and consider all aspects of the business. If you feel you aren't great at something, then don't hesitate to hire it out.

Think in terms of time spent on activities and you'll manage to run a successful business no matter the market conditions.

Cash Flow Delays

Here's something that an employee driver never has to deal with: customers not paying on time. The shipping business relies on thin margins. This means that everyone else is running on credit cycles and that makes you collateral damage at times. The manufacturer pays the shipper after 30 days and the shipper in turn pays you after 60 days. If the manufacturer delays payment, you don't receive your payment on time.

There's little that owner-operators can do in these circumstances. Invoice factoring— where you sell your invoices to factoring companies at a discount—is a solution but you cannot do this over the long term without suffering serious shortfalls. For instance, you'll have to discount your invoices by at least five percent to ten percent and over ten invoices, you'll have earned close to one hundred percent less than what you ought to have received.

Having a cash buffer (there it is again!) is the best way to deal with these situations. It's near impossible to account for every situation that might put a dent in your cash flow but this doesn't mean you shouldn't try. Rig maintenance often hurts cash flow and this pushes truckers to accept steep discounts on their invoices.

Doing this in an emergency is understandable. Just don't make this a standard business practice. It is important to understand credit cycles in this business. Many new owner-operators are surprised that their invoices don't get honored immediately. It isn't personal. It takes, on average, thirty to sixty days for invoices to be paid.

Time Management

If there's one skill you'll learn by running your own business, it's learning to manage your time. It isn't uncommon to see new owner-operators running around with a harried look on their faces as they try to keep pace with their schedules. Delays occur when you least expect them and scheduling jobs close to one another is asking for trouble.

A lot of this occurs due to ignorance or a misguided belief that you need to work all of the time. It's tempting to take on as many jobs as possible but remember that you need to account for unloading times and for unexpected events along the way. For instance, if you suffer a puncture, you need to have enough of a buffer to still deliver your loads on time.

At first, this will seem like an impossible task. However, time management is a skill you will learn with experience. It's unfortunate that no one can teach this skill from a book or out of the box. You'll simply have to experience it for yourself and learn from the early lessons.

It's best to remain aware of this challenge and watch out for it. Do your best at all times but remember that your plans might fail at some point, which will leave you scrambling to mitigate losses. Accept that you might have to eat a late delivery penalty at some point. It will make it easier to deal with when it does occur.

Finding Loads

As an employee, you don't have to ever worry about finding new loads. The company allocates them to you and all you do is drive. Sure, you drive a lot, but once you become an owner-operator, you'll understand why your company was insistent on fixing the number of runs they did.

A big part of being an owner-operator is finding loads for yourself. You cannot rely on someone else to bring work to you. You need to go out and find customers for yourself. Networking and planning loads ahead of schedule play a huge role in determining the success of your business.

Many owner-operators struggle with this aspect of business ownership since they're more suited to driving. However, to succeed, you're going to have to embrace this part of the job. You will need to reach out to people and let them know that you're available for work. Often, you'll have to do this while you're on a job. You can't answer the phone when driving, so you'll have to schedule rest stops for when you'll answer calls and respond to messages.

Being a business owner is more than a full-time job. It's your life. There will be no separation between what you do and your personal life. You will need to figure out how to integrate your work with your lifestyle to balance everything. It's a lot like solving a math problem while juggling three plates. It sounds impossible at first but trust me, you'll get there.

Preparation is the key to success. It's why I've adopted a slightly negative tone throughout this section. I want you to be as prepared for the worst case scenarios as possible. When they do occur, they won't surprise you as much and you'll have time to prepare yourself in advance.

Why Trucking Businesses Fail

The sad reality is that the majority of owner-operators end up failing at their businesses. The typical journey they take is to move enthusiastically into the owner-operator world, find that it's much tougher than they anticipated, and they end up closing shop within a couple years.

In this business, learning what *not* to do is just as important as learning what *to* do. So with that in mind, here are the leading reasons trucking businesses fail.

Failure to Plan

Failing to plan is planning to fail. It's a well known maxim but it's surprising how often people end up ignoring it. It's great that you're enthusiastic about becoming a business owner. However, enthusiasm alone doesn't ensure you'll get clients or receive cash. You need to plan everything as much as possible.

This is why time management is so important. There will be times when you'll be exhausted and will want to rest. The common narrative is that business owners should push through these times no matter what and get things done. This is utter nonsense. Always make sure you're well-rested and fresh.

If not, you're jeopardizing your business' prospects. Remember you have to drive, as well. It doesn't make sense to stay up all night working on your business when you need to be sleeping. Yes, there will be times when you'll have to sacrifice some sleep but don't make it a habit.

The common narrative of the sleepless entrepreneur is a myth. It often occurs with people who don't plan their schedules and end up doing everything haphazardly. Learning to work smart is a fundamental skill and nowhere is this more important than in the owner-operator world.

So plan everything as much as you can. Make peace with the fact that even after you plan everything out, you're not going to be able to account for the unexpected. This only means your plans need to be robust and flexible. Take the time to educate yourself, have low expectations but high hopes, and you'll be just fine!

Poor Management

Running a business is quite different from setting one up. In the United States, it takes less than 24 hours to get a company up and running. However, most business owners neglect the small details and end up running their businesses into the ground. Poor management in the owner-operator world often results in missed loads, poor scheduling, and a feast/famine routine that leaves you drained.

What compounds the problem is that you might be a very successful owner-operator but might struggle to scale your business. Many successful owner-operators try to scale their business but fail to do so because they don't take the time to educate themselves. You're a one-man shop as an owner-operator and this suits some people perfectly.

It's natural to want to make more money by scaling up. However, just like how you're educating yourself right now, you need to prepare to scale. You have to design processes and make sure you hire the right employees. Many owner-operators think scaling is easy and is simply an extension of what they're already doing. This is far from the truth.

In fact, scaling is tough and it's akin to starting a whole new business, albeit one in the same field. So never underestimate what it takes to run a business. There are always surprises around the corner and you have to account for them at all times.

Failing to Account for Critical Costs

The thing about running a business is that your expenses don't always happen in a predictable manner. They come in fits and starts. Just when you think you've managed to make a really good profit, expenses can hit and eat into your profits. Maintenance is a good example of this.

Most owner-operators rely on their rig's warranty to bail them out of maintenance expenses when things go wrong. This is a good tactic when you're still covered but eventually, you're going to have to pay for it out of pocket. There are many ways you can set aside cash to account for expenses. However, most owners don't do this.

They get used to having a warranty to cover everything and realize that they don't have cash when the time comes. This puts them in a hole and it leads them to take more jobs than they can handle. Again, you can see how careful planning helps you prevent such situations. It's so important to always have a solid cash buffer in the bank and don't rush to spend everything you earn.

That's just common sense. Unfortunately, it goes out of the window in the rush of making money. Always keep costs in mind and prepare for unexpected ones by leaving cash in the bank at all times. That way, you're not going to be blindsided.

Cash Mismanagement

A close cousin of failing to account for critical costs is mismanaging cash flow. Admittedly, this isn't an easy thing to do. As a business owner, you're going to have multiple cash inflows and multiple outflows, all of them hitting at different times. Often, it can be a case of skirting a fine line between payments to keep your business afloat.

A fact you need to understand is that the economics aren't in your favor. You're going to have to pay out of pocket to deliver a load and will get paid for it 60 days later This creates a two-month lag in cash flow at the very least. Throw in the inevitable deadbeat clients you'll have and you're going to be staring at a cash flow hole of 90 days or more.

There's no single good way to prepare for this. Invoice factoring is a good method to get paid immediately. However, you're not going to receive the entire invoice amount. Another method is to screen clients carefully. The issue is that you're going to have to say no a lot and this is going to work against you when you first begin. A new owner-operator isn't going to receive the best offers all of the time, so you're going to have to wade through the muck a bit before you work with top clients.

Even if you do work with great clients, industry conditions might dictate longer credit cycles. The best thing to do is to create a framework that helps you maintain steady cash flow. Utilize a combination of good marketing, invoice factoring, and a cash buffer to keep you going. Don't rely on a single method and account for future costs as much as you can.

At the very least, always have enough funds to cover serious rig maintenance. You might not need the cash at all times but if you are hit with a huge expense, it won't be insurmountable.

As I said before, preparing for the worst case scenario is a great strategy when you start out since you won't know what's going to come your way. Survive those first few hits and you'll emerge a lot stronger. If they don't come, then rejoice in your good fortune!

Charging too Little

This is a common problem I often see with new owners. They charge far too little and end up hurting the market for everyone else. It's understandable why this happens. New operators underestimate how much work it takes to run a successful business and once they discover they're running out of cash, they become desperate and start taking everything that comes their way.

There are so many of these operators that it might seem like the norm to undercharge for services. Resist this notion. You can charge exactly what you want and get paid on time. You don't have to compromise on your rates just because someone expects you to. I'm not saying you won't ever compromise but don't sell yourself short out of desperation.

Often a lack of knowledge of market rates leads people to underprice their services. This is why having a network of experienced operators helps. You can lean on them and ask them for advice. Experienced operators won't just help you with rates. They'll also refer you to loads that they can't carry.

So get to know the operators in your niche in the beginning and they will help you to avoid many mistakes.

Underestimating Compliance

This really shouldn't be an issue but unfortunately, many owner-operators neglect basic compliance and jeopardize their business. Perhaps it's the heady cocktail of setting their own hours and landing their own clients that brings this state of mind about. Either way, new owner-operators are very likely to ignore compliance requirements and suffer from penalties.

Aside from the monetary hit, it also damages your reputation. No large carrier will want to work with someone with a poor safety record. So always keep compliance in mind. The rules exist for a reason. They're there to protect you. So always follow them and don't try to manipulate them.

Failing to Adapt

Failing to adapt is a large umbrella that accounts for a variety of different things. However, the most common mistake that owner-operators make is to fail to adjust their spends and costs according to changing market conditions. Every sector changes over time and failing to adjust to new conditions only compounds issues.

Always keep your ear to the ground and watch for new events that might set off changes to your costs and economics. Prepare as much as possible and you'll be just fine.

The World of Owner-Operators

Now that you know about the challenges and the mistakes that owner-operators often make, it's time to dive deeper into this world and look at what it's truly like. There are many positives. You get to run your business the way you want and no one tells you what to do. However, you'll have to work twice as hard at first to gain traction and get going. You'll be an independent business owner but you'll have to account for every aspect of your business and be legally liable for your actions. This is something that often escapes the attention of new owner-operators.

Driving for a company rarely exposes you to the legal side of the business. Make no mistake, you'll receive a crash course when you carry your first load. The monetary rewards of being an owner-operator are excellent. You'll earn a higher per-mile rate and will be able to capture a greater percent of your load rate.

The average owner-operator in the United States earns around $141,000 every year. The range varies from $100,000 to $150,000. As you can see, it's a lucrative business to enter. There are many different kinds of owner-operators, all of whom structure their businesses differently. These are the broad categories of owner-operators.

Lease Operators

Lease operators skirt a fine line with regards to the economics of their business. Almost uniformly, their earnings fall on the lower end of the income range above. The flipside is that their earnings are more secure in many ways. It's a trade-off at the end of the day. You'll have less freedom but your income is more stable. So why is this?

The mechanics of a lease operator are simple. They lease a truck from a big company and contract to haul the loads of that same company. This is a good deal if the company offers a large volume of loads. Typically, these companies are middlemen and they offer large volumes.

The operator pays the company a lease payment every month and the company takes care of maintenance and everything else to do with making sure the rig runs smoothly. However, there are some caveats to keep in mind. First, companies rarely allow their truckers to contract with loads outside. This limits earning ability. This is the case even if the company isn't currently offering the driver a load.

For instance, if you haven't received a load for two weeks and are looking to haul, you can't contract with another company and haul their loads. Signing up as a lease operator with two different companies is unrealistic since you have to haul whichever load comes your way, assuming you're available.

Another point to consider is that you don't own your rig. Thus, your business doesn't really have any assets other than the cash you earn. However, your costs are lower and you don't even need an office as you don't require a marketing and sales arm to bring clients in.

In essence, lease operators are a step above full-time employees. They're in the middle where they don't fully own their business despite being independent but don't have to worry about the negatives that come with business ownership. Take care though, if you remain in this spot for too long, you'll end up experiencing the worst of all worlds.

This doesn't mean there aren't any positives to this model. If you're starting out in the business and don't want to be an employee, the lease operator model is a good way to get your feet wet and learn the ropes of the job. However, don't think of this as a legitimate long-term business model. Most lease operators tend to struggle to get loads according to their schedule.

Typically, the reason for starting your own business is to have more control over your time and choose your hours. Lease operators don't have this option since they're wedded to just one client, which is the company they're leasing their rig from. In the long run, you're an employee without any benefits.

Lease-Purchase Operators

The lease purchase setup is a step above the lease operator model. In this arrangement, the operator handles the financing of their truck themselves and contracts loads from a single shipper. Many new owner-operators end up falling into this model because their networks are initially small.

To implement this model, you can either lease or purchase your truck from a third party source and then book your loads as you choose. As I mentioned previously, new owner-operators may find it difficult to pick and choose loads because of their small network. Thus, it's most likely that they'll end up contracting with a big shipper and hauling their loads thanks to the steady stream of work that comes their way.

It's easier to come by loads with this model, provided you choose the right shipper. There's also no possibility of a conflict of interest between you and the shipper since they aren't the ones you're borrowing money from. The drawback is that you have to bear all costs of owning, and leasing, your rig, which calls for greater responsibility.

However, this is a smart way to go about setting up your business. The biggest choice you'll have here is whether to lease or buy your rig. I'll cover the nuances of making this decision in a later chapter. For now, understand that both choices have their pros and cons.

The only risk in this model is that you're still dependent on a single company to offer you business. This is mitigated by consistent marketing efforts and perseverance. It's a tough road initially but once you get going, you'll find that consistent work will come your way and you'll manage to divorce yourself from depending on a single client.

Independent Contractors

These operators are business owners in every sense of the word. They typically own their rigs and book clients according to a schedule that suits them. Typically, these people are experienced operators, even if they haven't been owners for a long time. This business model is ideal since you'll have the experience of driving a rig in an industry for a long time and can build a network to bring you leads.

Many experienced employee truckers go this way, even if they decide to start off leasing their equipment. While the freedom offered in this model is the highest, it calls for a great deal of responsibility on your part. Preparation, as always, is the key.

Company Drivers

Company drivers are ,of course, not owner-operators but it's worthwhile looking at this option if you're starting out. After all, it's best to gain some experience before deciding to strike out on your own. Despite the restraints that company drivers face, there are many positives that might appeal to you.

The only startup cost is obtaining your commercial driving licence (CDL). Your income is relatively guaranteed every month as your company takes care of booking loads for you and gives you a load schedule. Sure, you'll spend a lot of time driving but at the end of the month, you're guaranteed a paycheck.

This brings a high level of stability to your life and can help you better plan your expenses. If your family depends on you for maintenance, then such stability can be a major asset. The fact is simple: you don't have to worry about the headaches that come with ownership. For instance, you're not on the hook for maintenance or anything else that goes wrong with your rig. If this happens, all you need to do is call your company and they handle it for you.

You don't have to worry about booking loads, either. Your company's marketing department handles everything. All you do is show up and drive. Employee benefits are also a major attraction. You can count on insurance and other financial perks that won't be available if you're self-employed. In many ways, the world of the company driver is extremely secure and there aren't that many difficulties other than internal company bureaucracy.

Lastly, you aren't committed to your company forever. You can leave and find a better position if one happens to cross your path. You're not going to lose money in any scenario by working for a large company. However, all of this security comes at a price.

There is zero flexibility in the job. You cannot dictate your hours, your routes, or even your loads. The schedule your company maps for you might not suit you personally, but you will have to do what you're asked. Your equipment is also out of your control. If the company doesn't maintain its rigs well, or if the rigs are older models that don't suit you, there isn't much you can do.

While the income is steady, there's definitely a cap to it. Company drivers are paid on a mileage rate. Waiting time isn't mileage. Between circle checks, maintenance breaks, and compliance breaks, you're not going to get paid very much. Typically, this adds up to 20 hours per week where you aren't getting paid.

To make matters worse, you can count on being on the road...a lot! Companies earn a profit by putting you to work and you can bet they'll work you like a mule. Again, you won't have that much of a say in these matters and will have to comply with what they want you to do.

One of the worst things that I experienced as a company driver was having to clean up after someone who had used the equipment before I did. It doesn't sound like a big deal, but you'd be surprised by the amount of dirt and garbage a single human being can produce in a confined space. Again, you won't have a choice in this since you'll have to drive what you're given.

As you can see, there are pros and cons to being a company driver. The decision comes down to your priorities. Some people prefer giving up freedom in return for stability, while this doesn't suit others. Be sure to evaluate your options carefully and proceed with what works best for you.

Pros and Cons of Being an owner-operator

Now that you've learned about some of the pros and cons of being a company driver, it makes sense to do the same with owner-operators, as well. I've hinted at some of these points until now, but it's worth looking at all of them in more detail. The biggest advantage is having the independence to do what you want.

The biggest advantage is having the independence to do what you want. This holds huge allure to long-time company drivers who might be tired of the processes they have to follow. It's what everyone wants at the end of the day, after all. You can choose your own routes, your schedule, and who you work with. There's a sense of empowerment that comes from having the ability to choose everything related to your income stream.

A lot of this feeling comes from mastering your schedule. You can build as much flexibility in as you want since clients will typically trust you to deliver the goods by the time they need them. What you do to ensure the goods get there is your business. A few clients might impose conditions with regards to checking in on waypoints, but it's rare that an experienced trucker will be asked to do this.

Thus, you can plan your routes however you want and there isn't a company dispatcher looking over your shoulder all the time, asking you a variety of questions. As long as your goods reach your destination on time and satisfy the conditions of freight, you're the master of your time.

Aside from having the freedom from choosing what to do with your time, you'll find that you won't have to drive nearly as much as a company driver would. This is because there is no one else to cut in on your payments. A large company has costs and has to pay for ancillary equipment, which results in less money for you.

Owner-operators keep a much larger piece of the pie and thus, end up earning more by driving less. It really does offer the best of all worlds. The extra income means that you can invest more into your equipment and ensure the highest safety standards. Aside from safety, you can choose comfort, as well, as there is no one to force you to drive equipment you don't like.

Comfort is something that often goes unnoticed by beginners. You'll be on the road for the long haul and you need to get adequate rest. Comfortable equipment also ensures you'll be safe on the road. Driving a rig is a huge responsibility since you need to ensure the safety of those around you, as well. You're free to do whatever you please to ensure you're comfortable.

Some owner-operators I know bring their pets along for the ride to deal with the loneliness on the road. Having your dog or cat on the road can be a thrilling experience and will give you much more satisfaction. In my opinion, when you add up all the positives of being an owner-operator, it's hard to see why anyone would choose being anything else.

All of this flexibility and comfort does come at a price. For starters, you're a business owner and you're responsible for everything. By everything, I do mean everything. If your truck breaks down en route and you're going to be delayed, you'll have to eat the loss. Company drivers can let their companies know and the problem is taken care of.

You don't have that luxury and have to think quickly to mitigate your financial loss. Every second you spend standing still loses you money. This is why good planning with regards to routes and maintenance is essential. Another area of responsibility that often confounds new owner-operators is government regulations.

If you've come from a company background then all you had to do was make sure your logs were filled out and filed at the office. As an owner, there's an additional layer of responsibility to fulfill. You must ensure that you file relevant paperwork on schedule or you'll face penalties. You don't need me to tell you that those penalties can be harsh. Losing your CDL is just the start of it.

You'll also be responsible for sourcing your own loads and can't rely on a well-resourced marketing department to do the job for you. A company can employ professionals whose sole job it is to bring business in. You don't have this luxury and you'll have to do everything yourself. This means driving and following up with leads and executing whatever business development tasks you need to do. Over time, if you don't manage your tasks well, you'll find this a major hassle.

It takes commitment to build a business and being an owner-operator is no different. You need to show up everyday, no matter how terrible you feel. By showing up, I'm not talking about driving. You'll have something to do everyday and at times your to-do list will overflow. You'll still have to get things done on time since people will judge you by how reliable you are.

Even experienced truckers are sometimes caught out by their new responsibilities. For instance, they believe that their old contacts developed through working as a company driver will continue to funnel loads to them as an independent business owner. However, this isn't often the case. You'll be evaluated differently as a business owner and you'll find that old contacts will wait a while to check whether you're capable of delivering on what you promise.

If you don't develop a plan to handle your responsibilities, stress can get out of control and wreck your life. It isn't uncommon to see unsuccessful owner-operators suffer from the weight of severe stress. They mistakenly think they don't have what it takes or that successful owners are born different. Instead, it's all about developing good skills and habits.

You need to accept the reality that running a business is going to test you and that it isn't going to be easy. Let go of any expectations you might have of making a ton of money overnight and instead get to work. Plan everything and you'll find that money will come to you easily. One of the first things you need to plan is your startup capital.

If there's one mistake you should avoid, it's this one: do not go into business without adequate capital. You need to spend money to make money. Without capital or cash in the bank, you cannot operate your business and will have to shut down. Many new owner-operators make this mistake and enter without enough cash to back themselves up.

Aside from startup costs, which you'll learn about later in this book, you'll also need to set aside money for your monthly expenses and to cover any unexpected expenses. Do not make the mistake of thinking that your business will pay for itself from the first day. No matter how well you plan things out, that's not how it works. Always give yourself a sizable cash buffer and you won't experience many of the negatives that come with running a business.

A Day in the Life

So what's it like being an owner-operator? Well, everyone's different so obviously it's impossible to paint a fully accurate picture of what you'll face. Your day depends on what phase you're in. If you're driving or on the road, it's going to involve a lot of vehicle checks and making sure you're complying with Federal regulations.

Typically, this means setting your sleep schedule ahead of time and driving along your planned route. You should have a rough idea of where to stop and for how long before setting out. Generally, I have a plan but don't stick to it religiously. The plan guides me but doesn't impose restrictions on me. A lot of deciding when to adhere to the planned route and when to improvise comes from experience, so act accordingly.

On a typical delivery, I choose a route that appeals to me. I haul a mix of long and short runs, depending on the time of the year and personal events, so my days vary. On long hauls, I stick to delivery routes and speak to other drivers in my network for tips on navigating them. Communicating with other truckers at rest stops is also helpful since they'll give you on-the-ground information.

I set aside fixed times during deliveries to respond to messages and check email. I do not do this when I'm driving since it only results in me doing a poor job of everything. It's important that you take your safety seriously. This will do more to alleviate any issues you'll have with long hauls than anything else.

Comfort is also very important. I make sure my cab is ready for a good rest. Sometimes, I choose to sleep in a motel on a full-sized bed if the mood takes me. One of the pleasures of driving long hauls is that after a while, you'll end up running into familiar faces on the road. You might have run into someone in Nebraska and you'll run into them again in Indiana. The surprise is a part of the pleasure of this job.

Every once in a while, you'll run into maintenance issues. A blown tire, a malfunctioning transmission, or a broken light are annoyances but it's helpful to have numbers to call in case these events happen. It's a part of being well prepared. Short hauls are easier in this sense because they don't take you that far away from your home base. You'll always know whom to call and can handle situations better.

The downside of short hauls is that you'll run into more traffic, especially if you live close to a major metro. This is why I switch it up every so often. Short hauls keep you closer to your family but it's good to get back on the road to remind you of why this is a great business to get into.

You might be wondering about vacations. I often travel with my wife on work-vacations. We stop at scenic places along my routes and do whatever we fancy. That's the great thing about trucking. You're essentially travelling in a giant RV and are getting paid to do so. You can set your schedule and as long as you deliver your loads on time, your client doesn't care whether your wife or your dog travels with you.

Back home, when I'm not on a delivery route, things run at a different pace. Truth be told, I've never enjoyed the marketing aspect of the job that much, which is why I prefer being on the road. However, I recognize its importance, and therefore carry out whatever tasks I need to do. This means attending conferences, networking with people in the business, staying in touch with folks who I've met in the past, and so on. I always have a rough schedule planned out with regards to when I'd like to be on the road and when I'd like to remain at home. It doesn't always pan out exactly but I've earned enough trust in the business to be able to choose my loads.

In the beginning, this wasn't the case. It's best to say yes to everything that comes your way at first, as long as your safety isn't jeopardized. Just use your common sense and let it guide you. Some truckers I know get their partners in on the business and have them perform as home dispatchers. This means their partners carry out the marketing aspect of the business and they work together as a team.

Truckers who have been owner-operators for a long time and have lost the need to be on the road tend to farm jobs out and become dispatchers or shipping companies by themselves. This is a great way to transition the business to something that keeps them at home for longer. Ultimately, it's up to you to decide whether this sort of a business model works for you.

As you can probably imagine, a lot of planning goes into scheduling your loads. New owner-operators, especially those from a company background, tend to overload themselves. It's a nice problem to have and if you run into it, you'll figure out what your ideal pace is. A lot depends on the vagaries of your industry, as well, so you'll have to take that into account.

From time to time, you'll have to dip into the world of load boards to get work. It's not glamorous but if you need to do it, do it. These jobs tend to be rushed and generally, it's tough to achieve any kind of structure around them. So don't rely on load boards for consistent business. Use them to fill any gaps in your schedule.

Financially, make sure you connect with a good CPA who can help you prepare your taxes. Ensure you file all your paperwork and compliance records with the relevant Federal authorities on time. And finally, always keep tabs on your rig to make sure there aren't any maintenance-related surprises waiting for you.

Should You Get into Business?

This is the big question, isn't it? It's also a tough one to answer. The truth is that being a business owner isn't for everyone. As I previously mentioned, your priorities end up dictating whether this business will suit you. In this section, I'll break down this question into parts for you to consider.

Your Family Situation

This is the most important consideration, needless to say. Your family's situation will dictate whether being an owner-operator is a good fit for you. If you think your family is more likely than not to face an emergency, you need good backup systems in place. Unfortunately, this means being an owner-operator is a bit impractical.

For instance, if one of your family members has a health condition that makes medical insurance a priority, then sticking with a company is more beneficial for you. As an owner-operator, you're not going to receive the same benefits as those of a large company. Another point to consider is that as an employee, you can take leaves from work and still get paid.

As an owner-operator, you're in charge of your earnings. This means if you aren't working, there's no money coming in. Sure, you'll earn more and can save more money. However, if emergencies are likely to occur, you're not going to be able to plan your loads reliably.

Sticking with a company that has a reputation of providing great benefits and supporting their employees is your best move in these situations. Even if medical emergencies aren't likely to occur, you should discuss your move with your family. After all, they're stakeholders in your business, too.

Being an owner-operator means your cash flow is going to be less reliable. You'll need to discuss how you and your partner will approach this situation. You might need more savings in the bank or you might need to transition to owning your business in a different way. Needless to say, your existing financial condition plays a role.

If you've been saving up to put a down payment on a home, then switching to an owner-operator model is out of the question. You'll most likely scare the daylight out of your bank and your application will be denied. It's best to defer such moves until after you've secured your home. The same applies to any other major expense you might have coming up.

Generally, it's best to minimize upheaval when switching to an owner-operator model. This means taking care of everything else first so that you don't have to worry about a bunch of unrelated things to your business. Running your own shop is hard enough. There's no need to compound the issue by creating greater burdens for yourself.

The prudent thing to do is to sit down with your partner and take stock of your current financial condition. If you're looking at the owner-operator business as a way to get out of huge debt or crushing financial problems, then I'm sorry to say, you're not going to succeed. You'll be placing yourself under immense stress and you'll only make it less likely that you'll succeed.

Take stock of your debt situation and eliminate as much debt as you can. Make sure there are no significant payments coming up in the next year before you make the leap. Have enough cash to pay for six to eight month's worth of living expenses and an additional buffer to help tide you over in the case of unexpected business expenses. This might seem like overkill but it's best to be over prepared than underprepared when emergencies strike.

Commitment

There's no beating around the bush: you will need to give your business plenty of time to grow. At first, it's going to be tough. You'll spend 70 hours per week driving and will have to find time beyond this to execute all the other tasks that need to be done. It gets easier once you have a strong network, but it is slow-going at first.

This puts off many new owner-operators since they're not prepared to deal with the sheer amount of time their business demands. They believe that being an owner-operator is just an extension of being a trucking employee. However, as you've already read, this isn't the case.

I don't want to be negative here and dissuade you from becoming an owner-operator. It's just that you have to be realistic about whether you can commit to your business and understand that it's going to take you a lot of time to nurture it. Some of the less tasteful tasks that most owner-operators have to do involves marketing themselves.

I get it. You'd rather sit in your cab and drive all day long. Unfortunately, you will need to commit to doing things you may not like to succeed. In the trucking business, this involves figuring out your marketing strategy and planning your loads ahead of time. You'll have to follow up with clients about payments and deal with cash flow shortfalls. It's a part of the business. Look at the actual driving as a reward for your hard work.

The good news is that it does get easier. Once you've figured out your routines, you'll find that executing them is simple and you'll do them automatically. The best way to fall into a routine is to do a little bit everyday.

Some new owner-operators make the mistake of allocating all the things they don't enjoy to a single day and getting them over with. This is an instinctive reaction. However, it's not the right approach. To succeed, you can't avoid the parts you don't like. You need to execute a little bit everyday and keep chipping away. That is how you're going to be successful.

Your Experience

A huge mistake that many new owner-operators make is to open for business before they have enough experience driving. The trucking business isn't just about hopping into a truck and delivering stuff. Any driver who has been in the business for more than a year will tell you that there's a lot more to it than just that.

The best way to set yourself up for success is to be realistic about everything. This includes your experience level, as well. The odds are stacked against you if you haven't driven a truck in any capacity for at least five years. The reasons for this are simple.

First off, anyone who has been around for five years in any sector has a network they can rely on. Their network can help them land jobs in the industry and assist them in times of need. It can also teach them the tricks of the trade and most importantly, teach them which rules *can* be broken. It sounds odd to say this but the true sign of experience is knowing which rules are meant to be followed rigorously and which ones can be relaxed.

The second reason that experience counts has to do with the driving itself. Driving a truck on the open road is painted in romantic terms but understand that you're not going to be driving along winding mountainous highways with picturesque lakes and villages dotting the landscape. Driving a big rig is hard work. You'll have to deal with people testing you in traffic by braking suddenly or changing lanes in front of you out of ignorance.

Most people think a big rig stops and goes like a small car does and will unwittingly swerve into your lane, increasing the chances of an accident. As a big rig driver, you're on the road a large amount of the day, which increases the chances you'll be the target of insurance scams. Rear end a car and you may find yourself being blamed even if the person ahead of you braked hard deliberately.

Then there's the issue of normal traffic. Enter any major metro area and you're going to be surrounded by cars and other regular city traffic. Navigating this can be difficult and will likely cause you stress. There's a reason Federal guidelines mandate rest breaks for truckers. It's because we need them!

Every once in a while you'll experience a beautiful piece of road that you'll never forget. However, 70% of your day will be dealing with the terrible drivers around you and being blamed for someone else's mistakes because very few people understand what driving a truck is like. If you're delivering last-mile goods or running short hauls, it's important to understand the difficulties you're likely to face.

You won't hit the open road very often and you'll constantly be in city traffic. The good news is your driving times will be lower. However, there's a trade-off there that you ought to be aware of.

A big part of being a successful owner-operator is understanding how much rest you need and what a good driving time is. Everyone is different so you need to balance your needs with that of your clients. This knowledge comes only with experience. It's why I advise everyone looking to get into this business to drive for at least five years before even thinking of setting up shop on their own.

Dedication

Every successful owner-operator I've met genuinely loves the business. Yes, there are times when they complain about how tough things are. But this is just them venting. Deep down, they love the challenges and the various situations the business places them in. There's something deep within that motivates them to succeed at this business.

Everyone has different reasons to wake up in the morning. Some people get into this business to give their families a better life. Others genuinely love the traveling aspect of this job and look forward to hitting the road. The marketing side of things is just a tool that gets them what they want. And for some people, the marketing aspect is highly enjoyable and the driving is a bonus. Financial independence motivates them more than anything else.

The key is to determine what you love the most. All of us are naturally inclined towards something, so spend some time figuring out what you're most inclined towards and use that to motivate you. This will get you through the business aspects of trucking. It's important to tap into that source of motivation to be a successful owner-operator.

Some people are naturally excited at the prospect of becoming an entrepreneur. While many people like the idea of being one, not all are prepared to execute the tasks necessary to succeed. *Doing* is what will separate you from the rest. It isn't enough to simply want something. You have to go ahead and execute your vision. That takes time, effort, and a lot of patience.Ask yourself why you want to be an owner-operator. Go beyond just wanting to make money or the freedom of the open road. Tap into something that gives you a huge emotional boost and stirs passion within you.

Mechanical Ability

Every business looks to cut costs and trucking is no different. One of the biggest expenses you'll face as a rig owner is maintenance. They are complex machines with a variety of parts that can fail. If you've purchased a used rig, problems may crop up early in your ownership journey.

Savvy business operators know how to patch their trucks up or at least mitigate common issues. Here's where experience plays a role. Drive a rig for long enough and you'll get to know some of their strengths and weaknesses. You'll understand which issue is serious enough to warrant a visit to the shop and which ones can be patched safely by yourself.

These days, newer rigs have all kinds of electronic components and fixing them by yourself is near impossible. Electronics are finicky and cost a lot to repair. This makes it imperative that you have the ability to fix as many mechanical issues as possible.

While saving money is important, knowing which issues are large enough to jeopardize safety and the integrity of your equipment is even more critical. So don't make saving money your only goal. Prioritize safety and save as much money as possible at the same time.

Miscellaneous Factors

A lot of little things will contribute to your overall success in this business. One of the best ways of educating yourself in the owner-operator life is to speak to other people who have been in the business for a while. They can tell you exactly what you need to hear and will help you arrive at a decision, as well.

Being honest with yourself is a severely underrated quality. Many owner-operators kid themselves into thinking they have what it takes to succeed. In reality, they are enamored with the idea of being financially free but aren't realistic about the work needed to get there. Using your goals as motivation is great but you have to focus on what's in front of you at all times. This means executing tasks that aren't enjoyable and dealing with the less than savory aspects of the business.

Something else that helps people succeed in this business is being good at building connections. You don't have to be the most extroverted person in the world. In fact, many truckers prefer solitude which is why the open road has such appeal. However, you must always look to build and nurture connections along the way.

Truck stops are some of the best places to build connections. It's the one place in the world where you know you're going to run into people living the same life as you. You should always take these opportunities to build a network.

Strengthening your people skills will help you deal with clients, as well. You will have unreasonable requests requested of you and your clients will occasionally ask you for things that you cannot deliver. Letting them down gently while ensuring they continue to pay you is a critical skill that every business owner needs. Some truckers don't like this, which is why they end up turning to load boards. However, all that does is build even more uncertainty and unreliability into their business.

So take stock of everything you've learned so far and be honest with yourself. There's nothing wrong with wanting security and choosing to be an employee. It comes down to aligning your lifestyle with your strengths. Always check with your family before making the leap as you will need their support throughout your journey.

It's now time to move on and examine one of the most critical aspects of your business.

Chapter 2:

Choosing Your Equipment

Your equipment, or rig, is the centerpiece of your business. Get this choice wrong and you're going to enter a world of pain. There are many options for you to choose from and many methods to finance the purchase or lease.

Equipment is a major cash investment and your preparation has to begin well before you make a purchase. For starters, you need to figure out the basics about your operation. For instance, which industry will you support? This choice has serious consequences since it's your starting point.

Every industry has certain lane rates. If you choose an industry that has a low lane rate, buying equipment to support it isn't going to work for you. For instance, you might want to earn $100 but the industry supports just $50. Your equipment is now a sunk cost and there's no way you can turn a profit.

Your choice of industry also dictates the kind of equipment you will want to invest in. For instance, if you're going to enter the wholesale food delivery line of work, you'll have to invest in equipment with industry-leading cold chain technology. That adds a lot of costs to your initial setup. You'll also have to foot higher maintenance bills.

If that line of business is too saturated, you may then find yourself stuck with equipment that cannot be used for any other purpose. This is an ongoing concern for owner-operators who are in the hazardous materials disposal line of business. Their trucks come fully equipped to deal with radioactive waste but cannot be used anywhere else. The costs of modifications are too high and those trucks depreciate quickly because of this.

As you can see, you will need to think long and hard about the industry you want to serve. It's best to choose an industry that is exactly the same, or closely related, to the one you have experience with. Switching industries sounds great but it comes with a great deal of risk. Often, owner-operators switch their lines of work because of the promise of more money. This is a valid reason but the way they execute it is all wrong.

What they end up doing is jumping right into the new line of business. It is important to first build a strong base in an industry that you understand and then make the jump. This way, if you fall short, you still have something to fall back on. If you manage to land, you'll earn more. It's a win-win situation!

As a business owner, your job is to minimize risk. A truly successful business owner manages to make money while taking the least risk possible. In the long run, if your risks outweigh your rewards, you'll find yourself in the red when luck turns against you.

Another common mistake beginner owner-operators make is to think they'll start earning $100,000 or more per year straight away. This gets them investing in expensive equipment that doesn't give them a proper return on investment (ROI). Clients don't care about how shiny your truck is. All they care about is your compliance track record, specifically safety, and whether you can deliver goods on time. Sure, you don't want to turn up with a muddy truck, but don't think your clients care about whether you bought your truck used or new.

Choosing Trucks

Your truck (or equipment, if you prefer that term) is the most expensive part of your business. It's also the biggest asset you will have. Thus, you need to spend a lot of time considering which truck to purchase and how much you want to pay for it. There are many ways of looking at this decision, with the biggest factor being whether to purchase new or used.

A new truck is certain to be covered by warranty, which reduces your maintenance costs to almost zero. It's also guaranteed to have the latest technology, which increases comfort and reliability. And of course, there's something very gratifying about that new truck smell!

Used trucks bring different advantages of their own, namely, they are a great deal less expensive. Making the right decision can seem complex, so let's break it down a bit!

Pros of a New Truck

The biggest advantage of a new truck is the warranty period. You haven't been paying to maintain your truck (presumably), so I can understand if you're a bit bemused by my constant references to this. However, ask most owner-operators and they will tell you that maintenance expenses can be astronomical on certain trucks and having a warranty to rely upon can make all the difference.

Many maintenance issues arise due to a lack of proactive checks or a lack of knowledge of the truck's history. You might purchase a great-looking used truck but who knows how the previous owner used it. Modern trucks, even ones that were built ten years ago, have so many electronic components that it's almost impossible to fully check the status of a truck before buying it.

The best you can do is give it a look from the outside and examine maintenance records. You will be placing significant trust on the word of the previous owner. New trucks eliminate this issue and you can read reviews and conduct your own research online.

All of these advantages do add up. You're less likely to experience downtime and there's a smaller impact to your profitability. When you're starting out, extended downtime can make a huge difference. Imagine promising to deliver a load to a client at a particular time but missing the deadline. It's safe to say you'll have to work harder to make up for that shortfall and gain their business in the future.

As great as having a new truck is, there are some disadvantages. You'll have to invest much more to buy a new truck. On average, you can expect to spend over $80,000 on the purchase. Obviously, the price varies depending on which line you're looking to enter, as specialized new trucks (such as HAZMAT) can be in the $150,000 range, which is a significant expense.

This means that when you set up your business, you'll immediately be assuming debt. What's worse, you've drawn a loan on a truck that is depreciating the minute it leaves the dealer's lot. It is worth considering that assuming too much debt can have a negative impact on your business, which could potentially be too much to overcome.

In the rush of opening a new business, owner-operators may get carried away and make a vanity purchase. The reality is you haven't earned a cent yet and have assumed debt, which can be a debilitating move.

Used trucks can do the job pretty well. Remember that your clients don't care about how new your truck is. They're not going to award you the job based on your truck's features (other than a few basic ones relevant to the industry). For instance, if you're in the cold chain line of business, no one cares whether your truck is equipped with more efficient cold chain systems that keeps goods five percent fresher over 10 hours. Spending $10,000 for this feature is unjustifiable.

Adopt a business-like attitude to your operations and you'll manage to avoid overspending on features you don't need. For instance, if you're in the cold chain line of business, your client likely won't care whether your truck is equipped with more efficient cold chain systems that help keep goods five percent fresher over ten hours. Spending $10,000 for this feature is unjustifiable.

Pros of a Used Truck

Used trucks have a lot going for them. For starters, they are less expensive. Funny enough, some owner-operators see this as a negative. They believe that higher prices automatically guarantee better quality. That's simply not true. Yes, a new truck will run smoother but the marginal difference in performance doesn't justify spending five or even four figures in costs.

Many used trucks do the job very well and if they're well-maintained, they'll run for a long time without any issues. Most truck owners maintain lengthy maintenance records and you can have your prospective truck inspected thoroughly. It is an investment upfront but the cost of a thorough inspection is well worth it.

Typically, brake lines and structural elements tend to fail, so it is important to have these fully inspected. Of course, there's no telling how deep an issue might run, so there's always that risk. Still, the chances of buying a truck that has serious faults that would cause you to write-off your investment is low. As long as you use your common sense and follow your intuition, you'll be fine.

Another option is to buy a used truck from the manufacturer. These certified-used trucks are more expensive than the average used truck but they come with warranties that reduce your risk. You won't need to pay for detailed inspections and can hold the dealer accountable in case something goes awry.

A little secret that manufacturers often won't tell you is that older trucks are sturdier and run more reliably than newer ones. Their maintenance expenses are lower since they have more mechanical parts instead of computerized functions. For instance, in an older truck, if your transmission fails, odds are that replacing the differential and fixing a few drivetrain elements will have you up and running in a few hours, assuming it isn't a serious issue.

With newer trucks, there's nothing a mechanic can do *quickly*. This is because the newer trucks come with electronic circuitry that take up less space but are much more finicky. You might have to take the truck back to the manufacturer to avoid violating your warranty clauses. This means that if you've broken down in some remote area, you may be waiting for up to a month to get back up and running. Meanwhile, you're bleeding cash.

Used trucks can therefore cut both ways. You might spend more often on maintenance but these charges might be lower than what you'll spend on a new truck. It can be a tough call. However, the final advantage of used trucks ought to tilt the balance in favor of buying a used one.

Financing terms are a lot easier on used trucks than newer ones. After all, the bank is typically lending you $50,000 or less for these trucks and you don't need to worry about violating special terms. This isn't to say that every used truck has easier financing terms. However, on average, this holds true.

Given the lower financial burden on your business and the fact that paying cash for a truck and avoiding interest charges is a reality, buying used ultimately makes more sense. Used trucks also reduce the impact of making a mistake. Given the lower financial burden, you can trade them in and have a smaller loss in such situations.

Buy New If...

Buying new makes sense if you're highly experienced as a driver and understand the economics of the decision you're making. In some industries, a shift in regulations might mean that buying a new truck is the best choice. Typically, experienced operators also know what comfort means to them in monetary terms. Thus, they gain value even if they're financially assuming debt.

I must reiterate that this knowledge comes only with experience. You can't expect to drive a few miles in a truck and suddenly figure all of this out. Obviously, you can't ignore financial considerations either.

If you have a good sum of money to invest and are financially secure, then feel free to buy a new truck. If you aren't in this category, a used truck may be a better option. Make sure you purchase your truck from a reputable dealer or from someone who you *know* maintains their trucks well.

Many truckers do an excellent job of maintaining their trucks. It's also helpful to ask around in your network about truck sales. Someone always knows someone else who needs to sell their truck. You might even get lucky and buy a relatively new truck at a highly depreciated price.

Hopefully, your thought process with regards to used versus new is a bit clearer now. It isn't an easy decision, so be sure to take your time thinking through all of the possibilities. If you're still undecided, stick to buying used since the margin of error is much lower than with a new truck.

Types of Trucks

As you can imagine, there are many different kinds of big rigs, and not all of them are created equally. Much of your decision will be related to the line of work you're looking to enter. Next is a list of the kinds of trucks you'll generally find on the market. It's important not to simply choose the cheapest option, but instead find the best fit for your business.

Dry Vans

Despite the name, dry vans aren't vans at all. They are 53-foot trailers used to carry dry goods or non-perishable goods. They usually attach themselves to the back of a cab and are hauled.

Typically, they are used on long hauls and can be called semi-trailers or tractor trailers.

If your line of work requires a dry van, then your most significant choice in features will have to do with the cab. There isn't much to inspect with a dry van. Just ensure that the structure is sturdy and there isn't any rust of damage that could compromise your loads.

Reefers

These types of trucks are refrigerated and are used for cold chain goods or other perishable items. They tend to be the hardest to evaluate and most reefer owners prefer buying new due to the technology involved in the cooling process.

This doesn't mean that you won't find great deals on used reefers. It's best to settle for a used one if you're well experienced and understand how the technology works. You'll also need to have a sufficient budget for maintenance. On the positive side, the industry pays well and if you gain a reputation as someone who delivers on time and in good quality, you'll easily ensure a steady stream of work.

Flatbeds

Flatbeds are the most commonly encountered trucks. They haul everything from cars to construction equipment. Personally, I've seen everything from houses to windmills transported on the back of a flatbed. They're extremely versatile, so if you're looking for flexibility in terms of loads, they're a good choice. Their versatility also means you're more likely to land a load board job if you're looking for something in between scheduled loads.

Tankers

Tankers are specialized equipment designed to carry liquids, most of them flammable. Typically, HAZMAT trucks tend to have tankers attached to them. Truckers hauling chemicals and other hazardous materials also tend to drive tankers. They tend to be more expensive than the average truck but this is compensated by higher pay rates in the industry,

Much like with reefers, if you establish a good reputation in the industry, you'll find work coming to you regularly.

Bull Haulers

As the name suggests, these trucks are used to carry livestock and agricultural produce. Livestock can be anything from cows to sheep to horses. They tend to be medium haulers although plant produce might involve long hauls. If you're based in a largely rural area, then opting for a bull hauler may be a good move.

Auto Carriers

These are essentially flatbeds with specialized equipment built on top of them. You've definitely seen them if you've ever driven on a highway. They're the ones that carry two tiers of cars around the country. Auto carriers come in smaller sizes, too. For short hauls or consumer deliveries, a single flat bed is installed on the back of a pickup or large truck.

The presence of specialized equipment on these trucks confines you to just one industry and load type. Some owner-operators find this constricting. However, there are advantages as you don't have to look too far for work and standing out is a lot simpler thanks to your equipment.

Moving Van

The typical moving van is quite a common sight. However, this category includes larger rigs, too. Furniture transport and other household items tend to be shifted via these vans. You could also use a flatbed or a dry van for this purpose as there isn't any need for specialization. The separate category comes about due to the way the business of trucking is regulated.

You'll learn more about this category later in the book.

Container Haulers

If you're focusing on B2B hauls, then you're going to encounter container haulers. These containers are sometimes referred to as cans. Cans come off large ships or trains. Typically, truckers deliver medium or short haul loads. The way it works is the can is unloaded directly onto a flatbed and the load is delivered to a sorting warehouse that takes care of the last-mile deliveries.

Usually, the presence of a freight hub or a port makes opting for these loads an easy decision. Just know that if you prefer long hauls, these types of loads probably won't suit you very well.

Lowboys

Again, the name doesn't really convey what these trucks haul. A lowboy is a low trailer used to transport large construction vehicles or equipment. If you've seen a crane being transported on the interstate, you've seen an example of a lowboy. They are specialized equipment and have the expected advantages and disadvantages as previously noted.

Grain Haulers

These rigs are also called hoppers. Typically, they are used for medium hauls and their sole products are grains, corn or wheat. They haul these products from farms to processing plants and are typically located in rural areas.

Miscellaneous

There are many more types of rigs out there depending on geography and the types of loads they're hauling. For instance, you'll find rigs transporting logs and others with protective tarps on them. All of them have specialized uses.

Hot shot trucking is also a profitable form of conducting business. This involves hauling time sensitive LTL loads on medium-sized rigs to specific locations and customers. Usually, you'll be hauling loads on an urgent basis so the pay is higher, even if it is quite hectic.

Don't sweat the different types of rigs out there. Your choice should be informed by the needs of your line of work. Some truckers try to appeal to as broad an audience as possible but this isn't always the best thing to do. Situating yourself into a specific load type niche is a very good move. You can stand out far easier from the crowd and won't have to worry about competition.

However, there's a trade-off. If you delve too far down into your niche,you'll be entirely dependent on that industry and unable to pivot if things go badly. A lot of this choice comes from experience driving trucks. It's why I mentioned in the previous chapter that it's best to get into an owner-operator business after you've driven trucks for a while.

What to Consider

As I've been mentioning, the kind of truck you buy is informed by many different factors. Like with the decision to buy used or new, there are many factors to consider. Let's walk through them one by one to see if we can make this decision any easier.

Lane Choices

Understanding lanes is central to your decision of a niche or a truck type. The entire freight industry revolves around lanes. Truth be told, it's more of a consideration for freight forwarders and brokers. As an owner-operator, you don't have to sweat this too much. However, understand that lane choice can impact your business so it's best to pick lanes that make the most sense economically.

As an owner-operator, your lane is defined solely by you. However, it's not as simple as that. You might want to haul a particular lane but if there's no demand, it doesn't make much sense. Additionally, you will find yourself having to worry about interstate freight rules, as well. Federal taxes and state guidelines can increase your costs and make that route unviable.

The best way to pick a lane for yourself is to talk to those in your network. It's helpful to speak to freight brokers, as well, as they will have their finger on the pulse of how demand is unfolding. You don't want to pick the most saturated lanes since you'll face a great deal of competition.

However, you should also be careful of picking lanes that are too niched, as this could lead to there not being enough demand. Don't worry too much about this choice. In most places, it will be quite obvious which lane makes the most sense to pick. You can even mix up your lanes. For instance, you could haul full freight loads on some lanes but go LTL on others. The choice is entirely yours!

If you choose to drive long haul lanes then obviously, you'll need the proper equipment to do this. Make sure your choice matches the prevailing demand. For example, buying long haul equipment to service a lane that witnesses short hauls doesn't make sense.

Industry Choice

Aside from lane choice, your industry will also play a role in determining what kind of equipment you need. There are many industries out there to serve you. Again, don't think of this as a single industry you need to serve. Everyone needs a truck to deliver their goods and many of them have similar equipment needs.

Other than HAZMAT and cars, most other industries have similar needs. They require a flatbed and a cab to haul goods.

As with your lanes, your local area will often define which industry you'll end up serving.

For instance, the increased amount of electronics means that hauling sensitive electronics and semiconductor chips is extremely lucrative. If you're running routes in areas where there are manufacturing facilities for these items, you can make a good profit hauling them along medium routes.

Despite technology advances, agriculture remains a steady payer. Everyone needs food, after all! Just ensure that you have the right kind of truck for the type of haul you're looking to deliver. You can't show up with a reefer to haul grains, for instance. A lot of this is common sense, so don't worry too much about your choices.

Home Operation Zone

As great as driving on the road is, spending time with family and loved ones is even more important. Truth be told, this is the biggest factor that dictates the kinds of loads you'll haul and the equipment you'll use. If you cannot spend a lot of time away from home and away from your family, choosing long haul lanes won't make a lot of sense for you.

Sometimes, you might find there's a conflict between the prevalent lane demand and your personal choice to spend time with family. There are no easy solutions to such situations. It's best to conduct thorough research into lane demand before jumping into the business. Often, lane demands change over time, so don't rely on historical precedents to inform your decision.

This is where tapping into your network and having prior experience helps a great deal. You can assess demand ahead of time and avoid having to make tough choices down the road. If you find that there's a mismatch, you can discover this ahead of time instead of after spending a load of money setting up your business.

Experience will also help you to figure out how much home time you need and what kinds of hauls you enjoy the most. Take note that this will change with time. For instance, when I was younger, I loved long hauls and reduced my deadheads as much as possible to account for more of them. However, as time went on, I began prioritizing short hauls. Changes do happen, so you will want to be as flexible as possible when deciding your operation zone.

Remember that you can bring your partner along on your hauls. After all, you're the owner of your business and your clients don't concern themselves with who comes with you as long as you deliver your hauls on time. Planning these trips with your partner is extremely helpful. So don't think of home as being just the physical house you live in. You can take vacations *and* bring people along on your hauls!

That's one of the great things about being an owner-operator. So make sure you take advantage of it!

Haul Length

Closely related to the question of your home operation zone is how long you'd like to be on the road. I'm not talking about the number of jobs as much as the time it takes to complete a single job. Short haul truckers might be on the road for as long as a long hauler, however, they'll fill that time with multiple jobs. For some people, this can become too hectic. For instance, let's say you've delivered one load and have to immediately turn around and haul another within an hour, along with delivering it within 24 hours. That's quite a short deadhead time and it's going to affect your energy levels. Despite spending the same amount of time working and hauling, short haulers who schedule jobs like this are more prone to fatigue. Combine that with the usual city traffic that short haulers have to contend with, and you can imagine the issues!

Long haulers generally face more serene traffic thanks to driving along greater stretches of the interstate network. As a long hauler, you'll be driving across state lines and once you get to know your lane, you'll begin enjoying it much more. There aren't any differences between the number of short versus long haul jobs out there, so this really isn't a business question.

It's more about your comfort levels and what appeals most to you. Personally, as I've grown older, I prefer being closer to home. The trade-off is that I have to haul more in the same time as I used to spend hauling a single load. This trade-off is worth it for me, personally. You will need to decide what's right for you.

Long hauls obviously demand different equipment from short hauls. Your cab becomes more important than ever and generally speaking, long haul trucks have more electronics within them. This makes maintenance a bit trickier but it's worth it. Even something as small as a smoother gear shift will make a huge difference at the end of a 48-hour haul.

It's best to sit down with your family and discuss this choice. Remember, you need to prioritize time with them, as well. If you're finding yourself tired and feeling harried all of the time, you're really of no use to them. Always remember to prioritize your well being above the money to be made. As long as you're feeling good about what you do, the money will come. Obviously, use your common sense, but don't chase multiple jobs for greater payouts only to find that you can't sleep at night because you're too stressed out and exhausted.

Remember to schedule breaks from hauling, as well. This is something most new owner-operators don't consider. It's understandable why they do this. New operators have smaller networks and can't easily say no. Establishing your business is a priority but don't think you need to spend sleepless nights building it. That's not a business—it's a torture rack!

Instead, try to schedule a mix of jobs so that you aren't constantly staring at your clock. Try to work in as many rest periods as possible and you'll manage to make money *and* get some rest.

Truck Life and Use

This question is hard to nail down but it plays a role in your choice of truck. For starters, how long do you plan on using your truck? If you're buying used, for instance, you know that your truck is going to wear out at some point. You'll have to replace it at that time and incur a purchase cost. Of course, you can bank on business earnings to pay for additional expenses by then, so it's not as though this will be an unbearable expense.

Many owner-operators choose to buy new for these reasons. The thinking is that the lower maintenance costs along with the longer life of a new truck gives them a greater time horizon to operate with. This makes sense on paper but it isn't the best strategy in reality. For starters, the differences between a shiny new truck and one that has 30,000 miles on it are marginal.

Yes, the technology on the new truck is going to blow the older one out of the water! However, depending on the brand and the type of truck you're looking at, a used truck will last you much longer than you think. The key is maintenance. Proactive maintenance is the trick that ensures your truck will last longer.

Here's another thing that I've mentioned before but I'll say again in case you missed it: You need to tackle some of your maintenance issues yourself. You'll save a lot of money doing it this way and what's more, a used truck is friendlier in this regard. If you decide to work on a new truck, you'll void your warranty, as I've explained before.

There's also the question of how you'll use your truck. For instance, if you're hauling general freight, you don't need a heavy double frame. If you're hauling loads under 80,000 lbs, you won't need a fuel-guzzling monster of an engine. As you can see, it comes back to the industry and niche you're serving.

Overpaying for features you don't need is a common issue amongst new truckers since they get carried away in the beginning. Everyone is optimistic and the hopeful emotions lead to new owners thinking they'll haul every load under the sun. Positive emotions are great but you don't want to get too carried away. So make sure that you plan ahead of time and carefully map what you'll do and how you'll run your business. Your ideal truck will become an obvious decision.

How to Evaluate a Used Truck

A lot of truck choice comes down to planning. If you think long and hard about your business and the industry you want to serve, the truck you should buy will make itself obvious. In fact,

I'd say that if you're looking at a wide range of trucks and have no idea about which truck to buy, you've probably not planned enough. Take a deeper look at what you're planning on doing and you'll manage to narrow down your choice of truck.

That's the first step, of course. Once you've narrowed things down, it's time to choose a truck. Used trucks pose more of a challenge than new trucks, so it's worth taking a look at how you can evaluate them.

Fuel Mileage

Fuel costs are a necessary operating expense in this business. The less fuel you burn, the more money you'll make. There are many driving tips I could give you that result in less fuel being burned. However, they're easy enough to learn and you'll figure them out yourself. If you've driven a truck for three years or more, you'll already know what to do.

A truck's fuel mileage or economy is critical to evaluate. Your lane defines what sort of a mileage you can expect. Short haulers usually get lower mileage due to the greater traffic they hit. The exception is short haul trucks driving along rural lanes. Obviously, in those situations, traffic isn't as much of a concern.

Long haulers end up receiving mileage numbers close to the rated highway numbers provided by manufacturers. It's best to talk to other truckers in your network to determine what kind of numbers you can likely expect. The most reliable in terms of rated mileage tends to be Peterbilt. Of course, that's my opinion and you should take the time to do your own research.

Dig around a bit on online Facebook groups and trucking forums. You'll receive unvarnished advice about mileage and other numbers that will help you make a good decision.

Maintenance

This is very important when considering a used truck. There are multiple things you need to do to estimate how much you'll need to spend on a prospective used truck. First, run a history of the truck's VIN. If you're buying from a dealer, they'll usually run a check for you and provide you with a report with the complete history.

If not, you can use a service such as found on RigDig and take a look at it there. Watch out for the usual signs of trouble, including water or fire damage. Any structural damage will also be listed there so you can evaluate how bad things were. Combine this with the maintenance records that you will receive and you'll get a pretty clear picture of what the truck has been through.

Water damage is almost impossible to overcome because of the electronics that modern trucks have. These trucks will usually sell for incredibly low prices, so be sure to watch out for them. You'll end up having to overhaul the innards of the truck and spend more on them than the truck itself. Essentially, you'll be buying a metal piece of junk. With lights.

Fire damage is easier to overcome but if this is your first used truck purchase, it's best to steer clear of it. In fact, any major structural damage, major being anything that affects the chassis or the transmission, is a red flag. Experienced operators can buy such trucks since they have workarounds for them. However, they're not a good choice for newbies.

Take an experienced mechanic along with you when looking at a used truck. If the seller doesn't give you their maintenance record history, this is a red flag, needless to say. Some people worry about buying a used truck because they think they don't have the necessary knowledge. However, if you've bought a used car before, you can buy a used truck. It isn't all that different except for more wheels and metal.

Something else you must do these days is examine a truck's ECU logs. ECU stands for electronic control unit and these are the beating heart of modern trucks. They record everything to do with the rig and they're more reliable than paper records. You can ask a dealer or the seller to give you full records and examine them for any error messages. Check to see how these errors were addressed and whether they're still occurring.

Once that's out of the way, you need to look at what you're getting in exchange for your money. Used trucks have a rated horsepower figure and an actual one. Over time, a few onesies tend to bolt loose. Many owners will continue to list the original figure because few think to test horsepower loss. There are machines called dynamometers that help you figure out how much horsepower a truck has remaining.

If you're purchasing a truck from a private seller, you'll have to organize this test yourself. Smaller dealers will balk at arranging this for you or even question the need to carry it out. Don't take their word for it and go ahead with the test. The only exception is if horsepower isn't an important consideration for you, given your lane and haul types.

Arrange the horsepower test for last since it can be a bit of a pain arranging it. Typically, the cab is hauled onto a rolling road and the machine measures the engine's output while accelerating the engine to the max. Needless to say, negotiate a price based on what the output is. If a truck is older than eight years or more, it's best to carry out a test anyway as you might receive next to no power from the engine.

If a dynamometer test isn't practical for you, a simple way is to just accelerate the truck as fast as you can, within safe bounds. Pick an uphill road and test how well the cab accelerates. It takes some estimation since you won't have a full load to test with. However, if you've driven enough trucks you'll know what a good power output feels like.

We're not done yet! You need to conduct an engine health test, or as it's commonly known, an oil check. If you've been around trucks for even a few minutes, you'll probably know how to do this. Most sellers will offer this to you as routine, so check for any signs of trouble.

Another engine part you must always evaluate is the head gasket. A blown head gasket is going to cost you a great deal and there are plenty of used trucks that could potentially have an impending problem in this area. The problem is testing for a possible gasket issue is a pain and no one can arrange this for you unless you buy the truck. So what should you do?

There's a simple solution to this. Simply connect a pipe to the cooling system and immerse the other end in a jug of water. You'll see air bubbles blowing into the water. This is normal. Now, carefully disconnect the turbo and watch the bubbles. If they don't decrease in intensity and increase even more when you reconnect the turbo, you have a possible gasket issue. Needless to say, have the seller fix it or steer clear of the truck.

Something else to watch out for are emission issues. Typically, older trucks are grandfathered in when new regulations are passed. However, when the truck is sold, it has to comply with the new emissions requirements, which depend on the states you'll be driving and transiting through. A mechanic will be able to give you an idea of the emissions your truck of choice is producing. If you're buying from a dealer you won't have to worry about this. However, make sure you inform them of all the states you'll be driving through.

Emission requirements are becoming more strict, so it's best to avoid any borderline cases. Your truck will be grandfathered in but there's a limit to how often the government will let you do this. Many used trucks appear on the market because their emissions are wildly out of spec with regulations. Watch out for these!

Model-Specific Issues

Every truck model has certain issues that are well known. Without going into specifics, you can check trucking forums and Facebook groups for the issues that routinely arise. You'll have to check for these when buying a used truck.

Owner Information

If you're buying your truck from a dealer, this shouldn't be an issue. However, when buying from private sellers, it's always helpful to run a lien check on the truck. You don't want to pay for a truck that still has outstanding liens on it. For instance, the seller might not have paid off the financing and might be trying to use your money to settle the loan.

In such cases, they'll transfer the title to you after a few weeks. This is unacceptable. Always insist on seeing the title when evaluating a used truck. The rightful owner will have the title in their possession, so this shouldn't be an issue. Needless to say, if they don't possess the title, it's a huge red flag.

Sometimes, you'll run into owners who possess the title but the truck will have a lien on it from another party. In such situations, you have two options. You could take the one that results in fewer headaches and avoid dealing with the situation entirely. Or you could immerse yourself in the predicament and try to negotiate a settlement. In such situations, you can usually expect a huge discount since you're going into a lot of trouble to settle the issue. Often, lienholders won't settle but it doesn't hurt to ask.

Giving the seller a once-over is also a good idea. After all, you want to know why they're selling their truck. Most owner-operators are above board, but you'll run into the occasional troublemaker. If your instincts tell you that the person isn't trustworthy, then don't go through with the sale.

Look inside the cab for signs of how well maintained the truck has been. Smoking leaves a distinct smell that is hard to get rid of. It's up to you to figure out whether you'd like a cab that smells like this or not. Also take a look at the sleeping area, if applicable, and dig deep to look at what things are like underneath.

Dealing with a reputed used truck dealer typically eliminates these issues. However, they're worth taking a look at anyway.

Resale Values

This point is financial in nature. Your truck is going to depreciate, there's no denying that. If your equipment is highly specialized, it's going to depreciate even more. In these cases, it's impossible to avoid the financial damage. However, if you're buying a standard rig, you should seek to limit depreciation as much as possible.

In some cases, there's a trade-off. More luxurious models depreciate faster. However, if you're planning on holding onto your truck for more than six years, choose comfort above all else. Your truck is going to depreciate, so you might as well write off the purchase price. Besides, if you're going to be extremely comfortable, you may worry less about losing money on the purchase price.

Tires

Tires are one of the most important parts of your truck and unsurprisingly, they're also the part that wear out the fastest. Once you've driven enough, you'll be able to figure out what the truck is like just by looking at its tires. For now, though, don't worry about gaining these "Yoda-like" abilities. Instead, look at the tread and examine them carefully.

Tires that have almost no tread left on them are essentially worthless. You can subtract the cost of new tires from the purchase price and offer it to the seller. Another red flag to watch out for is uneven wear. This typically happens if the seller suffered a blown tire and didn't replace it on time. The other tires wear faster and the blown tire suffers less wear comparatively once it's repaired and reinstalled. Also take a look at any spare tires before purchasing.

Needless to say, drive the truck and watch for any evidence of leaning or listing. Sometimes, trucks experience what's called torque steer due to uneven treads. Press the accelerator gently and leave the steering wheel loose. If the truck veers off towards the left or right, instead of going straight, something's wrong with the transmission or the treads. It's not a serious issue but you want to have it checked.

If this becomes a bigger electronic issue, it's going to cost you a lot more money, so you want to avoid that at all costs.

General Body Condition

This is the easiest thing to inspect. If you see signs of rust or any other damage, ask for a full explanation and make sure it's been addressed fully. Be aware of any major structural damage and wearing parts. Usually, sellers have their trucks clean and shiny when you examine them, so make sure to dig beyond the obvious surface-level qualities.

Lastly, make sure the truck is comfortable for you to drive. Comfort is paramount. If you're going to use it for long hauls, spend some time in the sleeping cabin to make sure it's a good fit for you. Short haulers don't have to worry about this, but it's still a good idea to spend time in the cab and check whether it's a comfortable place.

The smallest of things will set you off. It could be excessively hot due to inefficient cooling or some of the buttons might not work and so on. Test everything and don't worry about coming across as difficult. It's your truck and money so test, test, test!

Must-Have Gear and Tools

Every trucker has a go-to list of gear and tools that they carry on them at all times. If you've driven for long enough, you'll undoubtedly have such a list, as well. Consider this section a helpful reminder of all the things you must have with you. The first and most obvious thing to have is a GPS system.

I'm not talking about Google Maps. You need a proper GPS system that identifies truck routes. You're not driving a tiny car that can go anywhere. Often, freely available map apps take you down roads that don't have adequate clearance of facilities. Even worse, you might end up being guided down roads that don't allow trucks and heavy vehicles to enter. Some counties even impose access hours which can throw you off schedule.

Most trucks have inbuilt GPS systems that help you navigate this minefield. So be sure to get yourself a good quality system or make sure your truck's system works, if it comes equipped with one. Next up, we have things that make your ride a bit more comfortable. This list includes items like your cooler, a pillow, portable toilet, indoor sleeping bag, a warm blanket, and so on. Undoubtedly, you'll have your own list so make sure you take those along with you.

At the very least, the truck you buy must have its own toilet and sleeping situation sorted out. Other features, like air conditioning and heating must work seamlessly. Over time, the efficiency of these features decreases, so make sure you test them out well. Coolers are especially important since you can load up on water and drink well ahead of time instead of having to stop everywhere to refill.

The other indispensable piece of gear you must have is a toolbox. Wrenches, screwdrivers, hammers, nails, wires, grease...whatever you need. Throw them all in there! Most trucks will come equipped with a toolkit, so you shouldn't have to add much to it. If not, simply buy one off the rack and add tools to it as and when you need them. In addition to a toolkit, you need a first-aid safety kit. You never know when you'll need it and you will realize its importance only when you don't have one.

One of trucking's nightmarish scenarios is breaking down at night on a deserted highway. In these situations, help will usually be a few hours away and you'll have to figure out ways of staying safe. Gear such as high-resolution vests, reflective clothes, flares, cones, and signs come in handy. Don't forget to carry along gear for icy roads, such as chains and shovels. Aside from keeping you safe, they also ensure that no one else runs into your truck or has an accident.

One item that I have personally found useful, but you won't find on these sorts of lists, are document envelopes. You'll be signing quite a lot of papers and will need documentary evidence of delivery and so on. Having envelopes is a great way to organize your paperwork. You won't have to go digging through your cab to find the right paper. Also, a well-organized trucker stands out quite a lot since the paperwork is much smoother. You can bet clients and shippers will notice this and send more work your way.

This brings to close our look at important gear and features to look out for on a used truck. For that matter, evaluate new trucks in the same way. A lot of it might seem like common sense but you'll be surprised how often it can be forgotten when the question of evaluating a truck enters the picture. Create a checklist of all these items and work your way through them. Be wary of sellers who push you to close a purchase or dismiss your concerns. Such people are most likely trying to draw attention away from the state of their equipment and are pushing you to give them money.

If the size of these lists concerns you, then consider purchasing a truck from a dealer. You won't have to worry about evaluating everything yourself and can rely on their reputation. It will cost you a bit more, but the peace of mind you receive will be well worth it.

Lastly, don't sweat it! I've gone into minute detail here to help you understand every possible situation that could occur. In reality, you might not have to deal with most of them. It's better to over prepare and receive a pleasant surprise than to under prepare and receive a nasty shock.

Financing

Financing your purchase deserves its own section given the immense investment it requires. As I previously mentioned, your truck is your business' biggest asset. Finance considerations also play a role in deciding which truck you'd like to bring into your business. The essence of this choice comes down to leasing versus buying.

Before getting into granular details, a few things that you must keep in mind before making a decision is the length of time that you wish to keep the truck; the special offers that are available; and any tax implications. Let's begin with taxes since they're surprisingly easy to deal with.

You can write off your truck's depreciation (along with any equipment you use) come tax time and this significantly reduces your tax bill. You can't do this if you're leasing a truck, as you don't own the equipment. Thus, leasing often hands owner-operators a double blow. Not only do you pay more to lease a new truck but you also aren't able to claim any tax benefits. It's why buying a used truck is often the better choice.

Next, you need to consider special offers. Holidays often means the rise of special offers and the trucking business is no different. Leasing offers are typically attractive during these times, so have a look at what is available. Remember that leases come with special caveats, so read the fine print carefully. Generally, leases don't trump buying a truck outright unless your ownership period is low.

If you plan on keeping the truck in your business for less than a couple years, it's better to lease the equipment. This is because you can access a better, and newer, truck and pay roughly the same amount. If you expect to be active in a certain lane, then you can put the truck to immediate use and make money off it.

The alternative is that you'll be constrained with regards to the number of miles you can drive the truck. This makes leasing a truck for long hauls a bit tricky.

Purchasing

So let's now dive into the nitty-gritty of purchasing a truck. As I mentioned previously, buying used is probably the wisest choice instead of purchasing a new one. Either way, the financing terms and related process are pretty much the same. It's just that the dollar amount connected to a new truck will be greater.

For starters, you need to evaluate the terms being offered by the bank and the dealer. If you're buying from an individual seller, then you'll have no choice but the bank to finance your purchase. A word of caution: Some owner-operators have the foresight to avoid debt as much as possible and try to buy their trucks in cash.

This can be a good or bad move depending on the state of your business. Avoiding debt is important but cash is the most important asset your business has. Let's say you spend $50,000 buying a used truck and your cash balance is now in the low four figures. First off, the amount you've just paid for a truck is a significant hurdle and it takes time to save that much money. You might end up not starting your business if your goal is to save enough to buy a truck in cash.

Next, let's say you begin hauling loads and are faced with a 60-day credit cycle. This means your business must survive for the next two months on little less than $2,000. That's a risky proposition. What if your truck needs maintenance or hits a snag? Unexpected issues occur all the time, so you must have enough cash in the bank to ride them out.

Thus, when you buy a truck in cash, you need to save even more money to make sure your cash levels don't drop dangerously low. How much cash you need in the bank depends on the number of loads you're receiving. Generally, it's wise to have at least $8,000 or more in there to stave off emergencies.

The other side of the argument also poses some issues. Let's say you opt to finance your truck. You now have cash in the bank but have a regular monthly payment that you must clear or else you'll lose your biggest asset. What if some unforeseen circumstance occurs that forces you to sit on the sidelines without hauling loads? You're now bleeding cash and nothing is coming in. You have to make those payments to keep your business afloat.

Cash management is the real lesson in all of this. While most people focus on whether to pay cash for a truck or not, the real question is how much cash do you need in the bank to make this business work. As I've mentioned, have at least $8,000 to help carry you through tough times. As for buying the truck in cash or financing it, it depends on your time horizon.

Saving money to buy a truck in cash is going to take time. Can you wait for that long? What if an emergency occurs that forces you to withdraw that cash and you'll need to start again? As a rule of thumb, don't wait around to start your business. If you've done your research and have completed all the tasks you need to prepare to launch, go ahead and launch your venture. Sitting around waiting for cash to come in is a fool's errand. The only exception is to ensure you have $8,000 or more more in emergency cash. Remember this is over and above any startup capital you might need.

If you're financing your purchase through a dealer, you'll need to put 25% down. On a purchase of $80,000 that's $20,000, which is a lot to save. Banks typically need lower down payments of approximately15%. On $80,000, that's $12,000 paid down. Interest rates from banks also tend to be lower than at dealerships.

I must mention that this is a rough rule. Individual circumstances will be different, so make sure you check all possible avenues before making your decision. For instance, a dealer might offer you a lower interest rate despite charging a higher down payment. This means your monthly cash flow burden will be lower. Make sure you calculate the full price you're paying, after interest.

For example, the lifetime cost of the truck from the dealer might amount to $90,000, while the cost using the bank's option might amount to $91,000. In this situation, opting for the dealer despite the higher down payment makes sense. Don't focus on the monthly payment as much as the total value you're paying after interest.

Dealerships will get you to focus on the monthly payment and will try to obscure the overall sum you're paying. Don't fall for this trap. Always negotiate the overall price and let the monthly payments take care of themselves.

If the terms from banks and dealerships are too onerous for you, you can explore small business administration (SBA) government loans. If you're a woman, you can apply for special female-owned business grants to finance your startup costs. This is not to say men have less opportunity. It's just that there are some programs specifically targeted towards women. SBA loans tend to cover the down payment costs but sometimes, they might come with caveats. For instance, the fees you pay might be greater than with a bank. SBA loans also have longer terms and you can't always pay them off early without incurring some sort of a penalty. The penalties don't amount to much, but they're a cost nonetheless.

Check with your local SBA loan center to evaluate the best offers. Remember, always choose the offer that gives you the lowest overall price. Ignore the monthly payment and just make sure it doesn't place too much of a burden on you. For example, a lower monthly payment might be great but if it keeps you in debt for longer while paying a higher interest rate, clearly this isn't a smart business decision.

If numbers intimidate you, simply ask the financing person how much you're paying in total. They're legally obligated to inform you. Pay attention to that number at all times. Aside from this, there isn't much else that happens with the financing process when buying a truck. You'll need to make monthly payments and can use the truck as you see fit.

Once your monthly payments are complete and you've paid off the loan, you'll receive the title for the truck from the financing company. Keep this document safe. If you're paying cash for your truck, you'll receive the document immediately. Remember to read the fine print in dealer financing contracts.

Sometimes, special incentives in the deal are offered only if you follow certain clauses. For instance, you cannot service your truck through a third party or you'll need to sign up for a special warranty to receive better financing terms. Make sure you understand what these clauses entail and never be afraid to walk away from a deal you don't understand or feel comfortable with.

There are many advantages of owning your truck. For starters, there won't be any mileage-related covenants like there are with leasing. You have full use of your truck and can do whatever you want with it. Just make sure to stay up-to-date on your payments. Financing companies usually consider you in default if you haven't paid for over 90 days. This doesn't mean you can fall behind without consequences for that period of time.

Your credit rating will be affected in the interim, so make sure the payments, which you'll negotiate by focusing on the overall price,are something you can afford. Generally, the longer the loan term is, the lower the payments are. However, you don't want to saddle your business with debt for over 30 years or some such ridiculous term.

The nice thing about owning the truck outright is that you now have an asset on your books and can claim depreciation to lower your tax bill. You can also sell it to raise cash, should you need it. You can also trade that truck for another one and refinance your loan.

One of the advantages of purchasing a truck is that your insurance rates will be lower compared to a lease. Despite these advantages, there are some downsides. You won't be driving a new truck and there's always the danger of obsolescence, especially in a specialized industry. The technology on your truck might not be compliant in a few years, which will force you to refinance to a newer option.

Some people enjoy driving a shiny new truck, so if this is a huge requirement for you, you'll have to purchase a new truck, which is a significant investment. However, financially speaking, purchasing a truck (whether new or used) is almost always the better option.

Leasing

Leasing offers a few advantages over ownership. For starters, you can access better equipment than through a purchase. Most lease agreements need very little money down and the monthly payments are comparable to a loan payment. In return, you drive a better truck. However, there are caveats.

The biggest thing to recognize is that you don't own the truck. The leasing company does. You therefore aren't free to use it in any way you please. You might have to stick to mileage limits every month or pay a penalty. You will need to service your truck at approved service centers and DIY options might be a no-go. It's a lot like renting an apartment instead of buying it. You get to enjoy a great place but you're not building any equity in your business.

Mind you, this isn't always a bad thing. Your line of business might require a newer truck and purchasing it might be too expensive. In such cases, adopting a business mindset is the best way forward. As long as you can afford the monthly payments and are making money in that line of work, there isn't any problem. Remember to include the cost of depreciation as an expense (loss) in this scenario since you'd be able to recover that cost in the ownership financing option. Note that you can write off the lease payment itself.

I understand that this can get confusing. The rule of thumb is: If your line of work needs you to have fresh equipment or technology, and if you can't afford to purchase the truck, go for a lease. In all other situations, purchase it.

If you decide to go down the leasing path, there are a few things to keep in mind. The first and most obvious piece of advice is to pay attention to the fine print. Lease agreements contain caveats that might make it tough for you to do business. Some of them can be negotiated, so explore all of your options with the leasing company.

There's a bigger risk to the leasing picture that many owner-operators don't comprehend. You don't own your truck, which means you're dependent on the leasing company's financial health. If that company were to go bust overnight, you're out of a truck. If this happens just as you're preparing to accept a large batch of hauls, you're sunk.

This is why it's prudent to examine the financial health of the leasing company. You don't have to be a financial expert to determine this. Instead, ask around in your network and try to evaluate what the general talk is like. A good way to gauge the health of a company is to look at what its employees are saying. Websites such as Glassdoor are a great way to gain insight into what the working culture is like.

If you hear rumors of cost-cutting or other signs of trouble, the leasing company might not be in good shape. A lot of trucking relies on word of mouth, so tap into your network, ask on Facebook groups, and so on. You'll receive good information from people in your line of work and can decide if the company is for you.

Another sign that a leasing company is in trouble is an aging fleet. If you receive truck options that are a few years old and are selling on the market for good prices to make a purchase viable, it's a sign that the leasing company isn't doing well. Strong leasing companies have the latest models in the fleet and tend to sell their older models quickly.

Inquire how often your truck (or prospective truck) has been leased in the past. A lengthy leasing history is a sign of trouble. After all, why hasn't the truck been sold and replaced? Aside from these signs, simply rely on your intuition. You'll pick up on more clues than you realize.

One of the easiest ways leasing companies get rid of older models is to offer lease to own programs. Generally speaking, these programs don't offer you a great deal. The way they work is simple. You make lease payments for a certain period (usually three years or so) and at the end of this period, you make what's called a balloon payment which is a large lump sum in cash. Once you make this payment, the truck is yours—title and all. If the leasing company is willing, you can even transition into a financing agreement and draw a loan for a year or two to pay the truck off.

Running through the numbers of such a deal is tough since there are many variables. Generally speaking, the numbers don't work in your favor. First, you're paying a lease payment that is primarily interest and doesn't count too much towards equity in the truck. This means the balloon payment is usually high. Instead of paying the balloon, you might be better off simply paying all that cash towards a used truck.

There's also the question of insurance. In the initial part of the deal, you'll incur greater insurance costs because you are leasing your truck. This adds to the unnecessary costs that leasing imposes upon you. The effective interest rate you'll pay will be much higher than what a bank or a traditional dealer will offer you on a loan.

However, there's one exception to this situation. If you have poor credit, lease to own programs are your best bet to getting your business up and running. They'll also help you mend your credit as a stable history of making payments will boost your credit score.

One option you could explore is drawing a personal loan from your bank to cover that payment hit. Given your improved credit conditions, you should be able to qualify for a decent loan amount at reasonable interest rates. If you have poor credit, make sure you talk to your bank and explore your options before signing up. It's helpful to draw the lease period out as much as possible and delay the balloon.

Note that the leasing company will let you draw it out for only so long. Plan ahead of time for your balloon and nail down the details of how you'll rustle up that much cash. Generally speaking, you'll need upwards of $20,000 or more to pay off your truck. Know where you're going to source it from and don't build pies in the sky. For instance, don't invest $100 in the stock market and expect it to grow to $50,000 to help you pay off your debt.

I'm exaggerating here but my point is that your plan to pay the balloon should be definite and reasonable. If not, don't enter into a lease. Don't be in a rush to jump into a business if your credit is less than perfect. It's worth taking the time to repair your credit and then do business. It'll be one less thing to worry about and you'll save money in the long run.

Scams

Special mention must be made of scams in the lease to own business. A popular scam that many truckers have fallen for involves minimum mileage allowances and forced defaults. Here's how the scam works: the company offers you a mileage allowance that allows you to make just enough money to pay the lease payments over the period and little else.

Once the lease period is up, the trucker can naturally not make the balloon payment and thus loses the truck. That same vehicle is rotated to another trucker and the scam goes on. First off, you'd think the signs of such a scam would be obvious. They are, to be honest. However, most owner-operators fall for them for two reasons. The first is a lack of knowledge of their industry and lane rates. The second is pure desperation and fear of missing out. Let's tackle the first one.

Lack of knowledge is easy to fix. All you need to do is review everything in this book and you'll be just fine. Speak to people in your network and ask questions online. There are no stupid questions. If people laugh at you, let them. You're learning and there's nothing negative about that.

As for the fear of missing out, this is a psychological trick. It affects people who have poor credit. In a rush to set up their business, they neglect basic financial best practices and assume they have no way out. The truth is you always have the option to walk away. As I mentioned before, if you notice that a company's trucks are being leased repeatedly without being sold, it's a major red flag. The buyout terms are probably too usurious and thus, no one benefits.

This brings to a close our look at equipment and choosing the right truck for your business. I haven't mentioned any brands or products here because those are my personal opinions. It's best for you to explore all options and choose the right one for yourself. As you can see, you have a lot to consider! Don't be overwhelmed by all of the choices that are in front of you. Take your time to work through the lists in this chapter and create a definitive plan.

If you feel nervous or are afraid of making a mistake, relax. Most of this stuff isn't that complicated. My aim is to make sure you're well prepared and aren't underestimating the tasks you need to execute. Feel free to return to this chapter and refer to points you're unsure of. Remember that as a rule of thumb, buying a used truck for cash or on as short a loan period as possible is the best choice. The shorter your usage period is, the more sense leasing a truck makes.

Chapter 3:

Finding Customers

Right, so you've bought your truck and are ready to roll. There's just one problem: You have no customers. Welcome to one of the stark realities of being an owner-operator. Many prospective owners get caught up in the positives of the owner-operator model and buying trucks that they forget to work on attracting customers.

Here's the simple truth: Marketing and sales are far more important for your business than what truck you're driving. No one cares if your truck is top of the line, with a few exceptions. Deliver what you promise and you'll have a steady stream of cash rolling in. Don't deliver and you'll be out in the cold.

Many owner-operators expect an instant stream of customers once they're open for business but this isn't the case at all. It doesn't matter how large your network is or how long you've been driving, you need to establish relationships and make sure there's demand for your services before you begin working for yourself.

Ideally, you'll sound people out much before you legally set up shop and ask them whether they'd be willing to hire you independently. Most people will say yes to this. Don't take their word for it. Ask them once again once you've created your legal entity but before you've bought a truck. I will explain this later in this book. If they say yes, then sign contracts right away and close on your truck as quickly as possible.

This way, you'll be ready to go immediately. Executing these steps takes a lot of planning since you'll have to juggle many tasks at once. You'll need to arrange financing and conduct marketing at the same time to ensure that you're ready to go immediately after your truck is in. If you're planning on switching lanes or industries, your task is even more complex.

No matter how hard it seems, this is the right way to do it. It minimizes your risk at every step. Most owner-operators buy their trucks and then start marketing. This approach does work but it's mentally taxing. What if no one wants your services or if there's a lull in hiring out loads? You're stuck with an expensive asset that needs repayment every month and you're out of a job as well.

Other owner-operators, usually unsuccessful ones, believe they can take any job that comes and earn a living from it. That's a bit like a new restaurant serving all kinds of food on their menu. Would you ever eat at a restaurant that served both Italian and Mongolian cuisine and claimed authenticity with both? Yeah, I didn't think so. You can't run your trucking business that way either. You have to niche into an industry and prepare to attract customers to you. A lot of this comes down to preparing a solid foundation that will keep bringing you work consistently. For long term success, you have to be strategic about who you work with.

Taking every load that comes your way will bring you short term cash but it has opportunity costs. An opportunity cost is the cost of something you give up. For instance, if you're faced with two prospective loads, one with a shipper who can give you consistent business and another that's merely short term, giving up the former load has a greater opportunity cost.

To minimize opportunity costs, and risk, you need to develop long term relationships. Keep this in mind as you read the rest of this chapter and the methods you can use to bring customers into your fold.

Single Customer Models

Take a look around the trucking industry and you'll notice that many experienced operators tend to have a handful of customers or even a single large customer. This is a great business model to operate by since it eliminates a lot of the typical stress that occurs in this business. The issue is finding a single customer who can give you consistent and reliable work.

There are many ways to go about this. Experienced truckers stand a better chance of landing such clients. However, the odds of a new owner-operator finding them are low. Chances are you'll have to wade through the muck a little bit before landing on them. Having said that, it's not impossible!

There is no secret to landing such clients, you need to reach out to your network and execute your loads as best as possible. Often, you'll be given trial loads by big companies as a test. Pass with flying colors and you'll find they steadily increase your loads until you become one of their preferred carriers.

Another way of finding such a customer is to choose to work with a trucking company. These companies will usually operate leasing programs, as well. However, don't sign up for their programs since this results in a conflict of interest. If the trucking company is leasing you their equipment, their priority is to first recover the cost of the truck from you and then give you loads. The result is that you'll make just enough money to make the lease payments and not much else. Never sign up to haul loads for a company you're leasing a truck from. In fact, never lease a truck from a trucking company.

Hauling for a large trucking company will give you steady work but it's not going to pay top dollar. This is because the company will take a cut of the rates from the client. However, there's a lot to like about this model. The large company in effect becomes your marketing division and brings clients to you. The pay cut you take is effectively your marketing expenditure. So it's a good deal in the end, assuming the lanes and load rates work for you.

Do note that you'll have to take a higher volume of loads than expected at times. The lower pay rates mean you'll need volume to hit a certain level of earnings. Still, it's a steady gig and you can earn good cash flow from it. Here are a few things to look for when choosing a trucking company to work with.

Owner-Operator Experience

A sign of a strong trucking company is the number of experienced owner-operators that work for them. An experienced owner-operator knows the business well and if the company is bad, you can bet they won't stay around! The greater the number of experienced operators, the better.

This will also give you access to a good network of people to tap into and you'll learn more about the business.

Flexibility

You're an independent business owner—never forget that. I'm mentioning this because in the rush to satisfy clients, many new owners take on too many loads and forget to arrange flexible schedules. They feel indebted to clients and say yes to everything. Trucking companies take advantage of this and this results in lower rates and higher volumes.

One of the reasons people set up their own business is to achieve greater flexibility in their lives. Always work with a trucking company that allows you to choose your lanes and loads. When you approach them the first time, odds are good that the company will push the perk of flexibility. However, there aren't many companies that follow through with this. Speak to their existing drivers and figure out what the environment is like. If the company is pushy and forces drivers to haul freight they aren't keen on, it's a sign that the company is having trouble signing clients up for their services.

Always prioritize your schedule first. If the company doesn't accommodate you taking time off or doesn't allow you to choose your time off, then run as far away as possible. Use your common sense here. Every company will have its needs and you'll have to work according to their schedule to a certain extent.

However, if they treat you like they would an employee then clearly, they don't respect you as a business owner. So it's best to walk away from such situations. Prioritize your time above all else and remember that you can always find more clients if needed.

Rates

You're hauling loads to get paid and that's the bottom line. Check around to see which company pays the highest rates. As a new owner-operator, you might not qualify for the highest rates immediately. However, don't think this means you have to settle for the lowest rates out there. You can always negotiate rates and loads. If the company seems unwilling to do this, then walk away.

Check to see if the company compensates drivers for working out of schedule. Often, these companies have loads coming in at the last moment and they run out of truckers to contract to. In such cases, it's perfectly valid to ask for a higher than usual rate since you're working out of schedule.

Flexibility is what it comes back to. The more flexible a company is in their negotiating strategy, the better the deal is for you. Never assume you have the weaker hand in these negotiations. The company will always push load volumes as a bargaining chip. However, those load volumes are only on paper. If truckers weren't around to haul those loads, no one gets paid.

Ultimately, these companies need truckers and the services you offer to satisfy their customers. They need you, not the other way around. So negotiate with this in mind and don't be afraid of walking away.

Freight Brokers

Freight brokerage has traditionally existed in the trucking business in an enterprise form. Typical freight brokers were large corporations filled with fast talking salespeople who didn't really care about you or your business. Sure, there were exceptions but there wasn't a huge difference between a freight broker and a stockbroker.

Older owner-operators still stick to this view but in my opinion, things are changing. Freight brokerage is becoming a smaller business thanks to the internet. Load boards are almost entirely online now and networking is online as well. This means, a prospective freight broker doesn't need a large office with phone lines to get in touch with prospective clients.

All of this means that as a trucker, you have a bevy of choices when it comes to selecting the freight broker you'd like to work with. First off, what do freight brokers do? Simply put, they connect clients to you and charge a commission for it. It's a lot like what large trucking companies do, except freight brokers don't own trucks or too many physical assets in their businesses.

Despite the impersonal nature of large freight brokers, there are advantages to working with them. Volumes are the primary advantage. They can give you lots of work and will have a steady load flow. The downside is they're not wedded to you. The freight broker is in the game to earn a commission. The more you charge for your services, the less they earn.

Thus, it isn't uncommon for a freight broker to verbally agree to giving you the contract but at the last minute, you'll find the load going to someone else because the other person quoted less than you. It isn't very ethical but it's how the business works. As you can see, I'm not the biggest fan of freight brokers. However, there are many owner-operators who swear by them.

It comes down to the quality of the relationship you have with them. Often, you'll find that experienced freight brokers will set up shop on their own and become freight broker owner-operators, so to speak. Working with these people is a good option since you'll be their first trucker, or close to it. You're more likely to develop a strong working relationship with them and gain steady loads.

Never depend entirely on a freight broker for your loads, no matter how reliable they are. They're in the business for higher commissions and you'll be on thin ice all the time. The moment someone with a lower rate emerges, you'll lose the load. Sure, the broker has to deal with clients in case the delivery quality is subpar. However, in most cases the brokers don't really care about what the client has to say.

After all, when you deliver loads, you'll be the one facing the client. The broker deals with everything on the phone and can always switch to someone else. This happens quite a lot with the bigger shops. It's why working with a smaller broker is a good choice. The frequency of jobs you get might be lower, but you'll be able to sustain the relationship for longer.

While the broker's quality is important, take note of the kinds of clients they're sending your way too. There's no shortage of deadbeats out there and they tend to be the easiest clients to sign. This is because no one else wants to work with them. Freight brokers usually sign these clients on because all they're doing is making a commission. The trucker is the one who has to deal with the client.

Another thing to remember with freight brokers is that your payment cycles will be longer. The broker is subject to the 60 day cycle from most clients and they'll impose an additional 30 day cycle to pay you. Do not accept these terms under any circumstances. Good freight brokers contract invoice factoring companies to pay their truckers. So it's not as if the broker doesn't have any options here.

Always work with brokers who factor their invoices because that's the only way they'll pay you within 30 to 60 days. Talk to other truckers who have worked with a broker and inquire about payment cycles. The shorter the cycle the better. Mind you, working with a broker who pays you within a week or some ridiculously short time frame isn't a good idea either.

It means they're discounting their invoices by a lot and are running a loss. In the long run, such shops won't survive. Aside from credit cycles, many of the criteria that apply to large trucking companies apply to freight brokers as well. Look for brokers who are willing to accommodate your schedule and don't accept higher volumes as compensation for ridiculously low rates.

Most brokers will negotiate rates for you so you're dependent on their abilities to run a successful business. You'll need to judge for yourself whether a broker is capable of doing this or not. A good rule of thumb is if you can see yourself getting along with the person outside of your business, you'll probably work well with them. I'm not saying you need to become great friends with your broker. In fact, you'll probably never see most brokers in real life.

However, use your intuition of what kind of a person the broker is and whether your business values align with theirs. If not, walk away and find someone else to work with. Larger brokers offer volumes but the rates they pay you will be lower. You'll never build a relationship with them. Take the odd job from them but never depend on them.

Smaller brokers are better but you'll need to evaluate how sound their business acumen is. So take your time evaluating your broker and don't rush into anything. Remember, they need you, not the other way around.

Dispatchers

While large trucking companies and freight brokers sit in the middle and find clients for you, a truck dispatching service, or a dispatcher, is slightly different. They're more back-office task oriented which brings a ton of benefits to owner-operators. Dispatchers occupy a curious space in the market. For starters, they aren't brokers but charge a commission anyway.

What they do is put you in touch with shippers and brokers. Typically, dispatchers work within these organizations but thanks to the internet, they've long since ventured out on their own. Large shipping operations have their own dispatching unit. However, it's possible to work with dispatchers who run their own shop.

To increase the value of the services they offer, dispatchers offer other back office services as well, such as bookkeeping and accounting. A particularly helpful service some dispatchers offer is to collect payments for you. Personally, this is one of the least tasteful tasks in my trucking business, so I find it particularly useful to outsource.

A good dispatching service will organize your invoices and follow up with clients as necessary. You can focus on getting more clients and delivering loads. It helps the most when you're on the road and are expecting a payment or handling a dispute with a customer.

Dispatchers aren't a one-stop solution to attracting customers to your business. At best, they'll put you in touch with other people who can do this for you. However, in terms of organizing your load schedules and other back office tasks. they add a lot of value. They might not be the ideal marketing and sales solution for your business but they do have a lot to offer. Think of them as an entire package instead of just a marketing arm.

Load Boards

Load boards are both my favorite and least favorite way of finding work. This might seem confusing to you but experienced owner-operators will tell you the same. For starters, load boards are places that connect shippers with truckers. They're a great way of finding work since they're a giant online marketplace that involves everyone in the industry.

A typical load board will list all available jobs and truckers bid on them. The customer chooses who to contract for the job and that's all there is to it! The negotiations for the job take place either through the portal, for bigger load boards, or offline. Many load boards handle payments as well, so both parties are protected in case of a dispute.

Many owner-operators, especially beginners, use load boards all wrong. When exploring the option of becoming an owner-operator, load boards are often touted as one of the best ways of getting steady work. However, this is false. There's nothing steady about a load board. The only party that benefits in the load board method of working is the company running the board. The customer and trucker both suffer.

So don't buy the hype surrounding load boards. Instead, it's better to be realistic about the role they play in the ecosystem and use them accordingly. Load boards are great for finding short term work to help you override any cash flow concerns.

They're not meant for client building purposes or any long-term strategy.

If the majority of your work is coming from load boards, you're doing something wrong. It's better to reduce the scope of work from there and instead focus on marketing yourself better. Use a load board only when you need a job quickly and need some cash flow coming in.

Most of these boards run off profiles that disadvantage the average trucker. The customer has just a few photos and a wall of text to go by and an inane star rating system. This setup favors truckers who were the earliest to adopt the platform since they would have received the most loads and ratings. The ones who joined later tend to be disadvantaged.

Smaller load boards don't even offer these features and you'll receive jobs at random. The only way to land anything is to apply to as many loads as possible and hope something sticks. There's another negative about load boards. They're a race to the bottom in terms or prices. Clients that visit these places are looking at minimizing price and aren't the highest quality.

Load board jobs tend to be ones that have been rejected by every other trucker out there, so you can imagine the kind of loads on offer. They either pay too low or the client has a credit cycle that's too long. So why should you apply for these jobs? Well, as I said, business is variable and random at times, especially in the beginning.

If you've been searching for loads for a while and haven't yet landed a great client, opting for a load board job can ease cash flow concerns. It's a good backup option in case your primary leads fail to materialize. When you first begin your business, it's good to opt for a few load board jobs to bring some cash in.

Despite the "platform" nature of a load board, it is possible to build relationships with some of the clients on there. Mind you, these clients will never turn into high-paying clients since the initial rates they paid you via the load board will become a standard. However, it's possible to receive steady work from them.

The average load board customer offers a one-off job and the pay isn't all that great. So never make it your primary choice of work. Once you build a reputation on the board, you can apply to the higher paying jobs and attract better clients to you. However, it takes time to build such a reputation and you'll have to haul all kinds of loads to build that reputation. It's advised to spend that time instead on specializing in a certain industry and networking within it to build sustainable relationships.

Direct Shippers

The best way to build a sustainable long-term business is to build a relationship with a direct shipper. These clients often assume a mythical status amongst unsuccessful owner-operators. Many owner-operators never get to work with a direct shipper and remain stuck in the mid to lower tiers of this profession, relying on freight brokers and load boards to fill their schedules.

There isn't a single method to locate direct shippers. Think of this task as comprising a number of smaller tasks that you need to do well. The effects of these efforts are cumulative so consistent effort is what brings results.

First off, why should you deal with shippers directly? The most important reason is sustainability and security. The average shipper has fixed load schedules and lanes. They have calendars that you can match yours up with and what's more, they pay well. You'll be dealing with the client directly and thus, there are no middlemen to take a cut of your earnings.

In short, you'll haul less, compared to the other options, and will earn more. owner-operators who succeed in this business understand this secret and always pursue these shippers as a priority. Remember that not all direct shippers are created equal. Some are better than others and much comes down to how you prefer to work and what your schedule is like.

This process is as much about you selecting a shipper to work with as it has to do with a shipper selecting you. So be sure to seek companies and clients that you would enjoy working for, instead of randomly selecting every direct shipper on the market. The following is some of the criteria you can use to screen your potential direct shippers.

Size

Size matters in trucking and logistics. The larger the shipper is, the more sustainable their business is for you. Smaller shippers often pay well but their business is intermittent. They simply lack the volumes you will need to sustain your operations. Mind you, larger shippers receive many offers from truckers, so you'll face more competition in trying to win their business.

Negotiations with these organizations can often put you at a disadvantage since they simply have more choices. Still, don't compromise your needs too much for the sake of landing a contract. There are many shippers out there that need trucking services, so it's not as if the current prospect is the only one that you will discover.

Some of the telltale signs of an established shipper are a good reputation and a well-reviewed business pattern in the industry. By well reviewed, I mean that there are enough people around that have heard of this company and have worked with them. And most importantly, have good things to say about their business principles.

Timeliness of loads is also an important factor. A good shipper has the right volumes to give you enough business but not so much that they're pushing you to take loads off-schedule at inopportune times. It comes back to them ensuring that they hired enough truckers to service their needs and planned their output well. Fluctuating demand for trucking services is a good sign of an unstable shipper. Feel free to sign up with them but don't make them your primary source of income.

Payments

This is the big one: What are their credit cycles like and how well do they stick to them? I'm not sure how much of a surprise this will be to you but most shippers don't stick to their credit cycles and delay payments. This directly affects your bottom line, so you must always check how well the shipper pays.

The logistics industry as a whole is a tough one and margins are low. Occasional violations of credit cycles do occur but you don't want to work for a shipper that routinely violates them. Check with your network to see how well the shipper sticks to their terms and conditions.

Needless to say, stay away from a shipper that takes 90 days or more to clear invoices.

Lane Availability

Lane availability and suitability is a big factor in choosing a shipper to work with. The shipper might tick all boxes but if they ship loads to places that are far outside your lane, there's not much point in working with them. This is a tough choice to make and personally, a little compromise is justified on your part.

For instance, if you've identified a great shipper that is close to your home base and know that they're shipping to places outside your lane, you might want to consider changing your lanes. This will require you to talk to your family and manage your other loads closely, but if the shipper ticks all the boxes, it's worth the change.

At the end of the day, your aim is to reduce the risk to your business. This means creating as stable a cash flow pattern as possible. If this means having to change your lane or switch from short to long hauls, consider doing so. You'll have a more stable income and won't have to deal with a lot of the headaches that come with running a business. Cash flow is the most important thing to consider, so try not to be too wedded to your needs.

Having said that, if you cannot make a lane change work for you, you will need to walk away from that shipper. There are many direct shippers who need your services, so don't feel like you're the one that has to compromise at all times. Give it your best shot but if you can't make it work, change your game plan.

Try negotiating with the shipper, as well, to gauge their level of flexibility. They won't change their entire business model for you overnight, but often, asking about making a change can lead to surprising results. Many owner-operators don't bother to ask, or consider negotiating terms. They simply take what's given to them and carry on. Asking for a few changes never hurts. It leads to a longer lasting business relationship since both parties will know exactly where the other stands.

So go ahead and negotiate! Whether it's payment terms or lane changes, or even enquiring about possible amendments to their lanes, ask the shipper openly and honestly. You'll often find them to be more than amenable. If the relationship doesn't end up working out, then feel free to walk away. After all, you gave it your best shot!

Service Orientation

When working with a direct shipper, you will want to look for someone who is the exact opposite of the average load board client. What I mean by this is that the clients you find on load boards are focused only on the price of your services. Good direct shipping clients focus on the quality of service and the condition of their goods on delivery. This isn't to say that prices aren't important to them. It's just that price isn't the only thing on which the contract hinges.

A good shipper understands the value of the service you provide and seeks stability in their contacts. This means that they understand your need to make money, as well. From their perspective, a long-term contract with a reliable trucker is worth its weight in gold. This is because, believe it or not, they don't get approached by many good truckers. For the most part, they receive bids from truckers with outdated equipment or who can't deliver loads safely and on time.

So always screen direct shippers like this and only work with the best. Don't focus on the volumes they can give you but on the quality of service they're looking for. You'll make stable money over a longer period.

Finding Direct Shippers

As you can imagine, it takes a little bit of work to locate and sign a direct shipper. In the old days, this was a tough task and a lot depended on the location you were in. For instance, if you were in California and there were no quality shippers in your local zip code, you couldn't do anything about it except move somewhere else. This isn't to say California has terrible shippers, it's just an example.

The internet has simplified a lot of things. The flipside is that more people than ever are reaching out to shippers directly, so it takes some effort and good luck to make things work. The key is preparation. Most truckers fail to prepare adequately before calling on a shipper via the methods I am about to outline. Remember, these methods aren't particularly special. In fact, all of them are common sense ways of approaching a prospective client.

How you approach them is the key. Most truckers reach out via a generic "I'm looking for work, you got some?" message and this isn't going to land you anywhere. You need to be smarter than that and project yourself as someone who they would want to work with.

Cold Contact

Many people dread cold calls and there are good reasons for that. It's tough to pick up the phone and dial an unknown number and hope to land a load. The thing is that cold calls aren't going to get you that far unless you're very lucky. The chances of calling a shipper and them requiring someone with your skills at the same time is minute. For the most part, shippers receive a large volume of cold calls and most of them are time-wasters.

So how can you stand out? Well, for starters, don't have high expectations. When calling a shipper, fully expect to be told to call back later or to leave a message. Neither of these results are going to lead to anything solid. However, your marketing efforts are cumulative. A single call won't necessarily yield any results. But once you pair a call with an in-person visit, a social media message, and a direct mail pamphlet...now you're getting somewhere!

This is the mistake that most owner-operators make. They try cold calling, get repeatedly rejected, and think that this whole marketing thing is overrated. You need to create a plan that has you contacting a prospective client in multiple ways. The more touch points you have with the client, the more likely they are to respond to you favorably.

Cold calling is just one method. When you call a shipper, ask to speak to the person in charge of contracting truckers and similar services. Most likely, you'll be asked to leave a message or be told that they don't accept cold calls. If you manage to get past these barriers and establish contact, don't waste their time.

Tell them why you're calling, what you can offer, and whether they're open to you sending them more information. Get their email address or postal address. Ask them whether they'd be willing to connect over LinkedIn. The purpose of your cold call is merely to establish contact and let them know you exist. They're going to forget about you in a few minutes, and that's okay. The key is to establish further communication.

Contrast this with the typical way that truckers use cold calls. It's often something along the lines of: "Hi, I can haul, do you have loads?", followed by a rejection and the trucker never getting in touch with that person again. You won't land a client this way. Needless to say, prepare beforehand and learn everything there is to know about the prospective client. This takes hard work.

This means that you need to speak to people in the industry and get to know what that company is like. What are their preferred lanes and how often do they have loads? You might not receive all the information you need immediately, and that's okay. The trick is to know something deeper than what's on the surface about that client. If you're hit with a question, you won't be dumbstruck and will know how to properly reply.

You may get lucky and have someone invite you over for further contract talks immediately. However, don't expect this. Plan to be rejected a lot and make establishing further contact your goal. That way, you won't be discouraged and will have clear next steps to execute.

These days, most shippers will tell you to send them an email. This isn't an accident. Emails are easier to ignore! Don't be discouraged by this. Instead, treat the email like you would a cold call. Emails require a little more prep work than a call since you'll need to leave a link to your professional social media profiles, such as LinkedIn and/or your website, if you have one. So make sure you set those up before you start contacting people.

It's a good idea to have a simple website that profiles who you are and the services you offer. It doesn't have to be fancy, just professional. If you don't have one at this point, that's okay! Just make sure you get one made up at some point. You don't have to invest in a fancy designer, just make sure it looks clean and that people can easily find your background and contact information.

Even with emails, make sure you're opening a path to further connection. Don't worry about landing a contract with the firm, simply ask to remain in touch. In fact, tell them you'll remain in touch periodically so that they know to think of you when a need arises. Never push for a sale in a cold setting. You'll only come across as difficult.

In-Person Visits

In-person visits are trickier to make but you can get away with them with smaller shippers. Larger shippers will likely not entertain you and simply ask you to leave some material for them to review. As you can guess, no one ever reviews those things. Therefore, when you're contacting a larger shipper try to set up an appointment via email or phone before visiting them.

With smaller shippers, walk into their office and ask to meet the person that you contacted. Once you meet them, continue with the "staying in touch" theme and don't push for an immediate contract. Prepare beforehand by printing out some material for them to review. This could be a glossy brochure of your services or a simple one-pager that explains who you are and the services your business provides. Think of it as a resume for your business.

Ask them pertinent questions about their loads and what issues they're facing. In fact, focus entirely on the problems they're facing. The more you get them talking about their issues, the more you can offer to help them out. It gives you something to work with, instead of aiming randomly in the dark.

Use your common sense when meeting these people. Look professional and leave the unsuitable jokes in your cab, as these people don't need to hear them. Present your best professional self and leave the rest up to them. Again, don't force them to make a decision, as this only damages your prospects.

Before the meeting ends, let them know that you'll remain in touch via email or via LinkedIn, or both. Get their business card and make a note to remain in touch with them at certain frequencies. This could be once a month or twice a month. You certainly don't want to be calling them every week or every day, as this can make you seem desperate.

No matter how desperate you really are, never let them see you sweat. It's fine to be nervous about these meetings. Prepare well before you attend and remain positive!

Mail

In today's electronic world, direct mail is viewed as an anachronism. I mean...who writes letters anymore? However, direct mail is one of the best ways of staying in touch with a client and advertising your services. Direct mail campaigns can be as simple as sending a regular postcard once a month, with a logo of your company or a picture of you next to your truck and your company's name. This isn't a travel postcard, just a simple reminder that you exist.

Direct mail postcards are inexpensive to buy and the services that organize it for you are equally cheap. You can outsource card design and mailing to a print company and they'll do it for you. Alternatively, you can hire someone to do it and keep things in-house. It depends on how much money you're making and what you can afford. As you grow bigger, you must definitely keep things in-house.

The electronic cousin of direct mail is equally effective these days. The challenge is to make sure you don't overwhelm your prospects with touchpoints. For instance, if you've cold called someone on Monday, you don't want to send them an email, a direct mail, and visit them in person by Wednesday. That's too much, too soon.

Emails are great because you can automate them and you'll need to craft them just once before sending them out. You should create an email newsletter (you'll need a website for this) and add people to your list. Don't add random people to your list! Add the people you've contacted and get their permission before sending them your newsletter.

You can send email newsletters exclusively or pair them with direct mailers. If so, make sure you send them a maximum of two mails every month. Any more and you'll overwhelm them. Your email newsletter can simply be a reminder of who you are and what you do. You can talk about some of the issues the industry is facing or some of the steps you've taken to address these issues and offer better services.

Mailers are extremely powerful because they establish instant authority. This is because only large trucking companies use them. Individual owner-operators rarely send mailers. Most of them stick to cold calling and in-person visits. Both of those techniques are hit or miss. You have to back them up with more solid strategies and touches like mailers and social media messaging. That's how you get your marketing machine going.

As you can see, you've already created three layers to your marketing. There's cold calling, followed by in-person visits, followed by mailers. The mailing portion can be automated so it isn't going to take too much of your time or money. Simply focus on being helpful at all times and never push for an immediate sale.

For example, it's fine to say something like "hire me" in your mailers. However, don't repeatedly say this or you'll turn your prospects off. Be patient and focus on remaining in touch. They'll automatically reach out to you when the time is right.

Social Media

In a professional context, there is just one social network you ought to focus on. It's LinkedIn and if you learn to use it well, consider it a superpower. Many truckers shy away from building profiles on social media because of the perceived difficulty of influencing algorithms and so on. This is the wrong view to take.

You can't influence or manipulate an algorithm, it's too smart for you. Instead, look to provide help and genuinely offer assistance in your field. You'll start getting noticed by people. LinkedIn also offers you a great way to professionally connect with others in your industry.

Instead, use your LinkedIn profile to introduce yourself to shippers and other people in your industry. You can do this by sending people a simple "hello" message and connecting with them. Make sure your profile is professional and has relevant information regarding the services you offer. LinkedIn offers you the chance to specify your job title and some people get cute with this.

Don't overcomplicate this and simply write what you do. In this case, it'll be "owner-operator" or "trucking services provider" or another relevant phrase. You can even join groups on LinkedIn that are relevant to your business. There are many trucking groups on the network but most of them tend to be bootleg loadboards. Don't rely on them for jobs but you can find other people in your industry there.

Regular interaction with people you connect with is the key to success on the network. Respond to their posts and comment on them to make sure they remember who you are. If anyone asks for help, offer genuine advice and don't focus on selling. Your aim is to layer your LinkedIn activity with the other methods you're using. As a combination, they're hard to resist.

The key to successful marketing is remaining at the top of your customers' minds. This is why a single channel won't suffice. You need to be active and constantly interact with these people. Over time, when they have a need, they'll remember you and reach out to you. Make sure you have your business contact information on your profile so that they know how to get in touch with you.

LinkedIn offers a few premium features, like sending mails to people on the platform. You don't need these features. When you first sign up to the network, you'll receive a complimentary month. Use those features to see how they work for you. Generally speaking, it's not as if they make a huge advantage for a trucker. What's more important is that you layer your activity with everything else you do and not depend on just one channel to get noticed.

Many industry organizations have their pages on LinkedIn so make sure you reach out to people connected to them. Once someone connects with you, you can view their connections and find even more people. Be patient with LinkedIn and you'll find work coming in regularly over time. It's a snowball that takes time to grow. Persistence is the key and don't worry about "working" the algorithm.

Simply be professional and helpful, and everything else will take care of itself.

Conferences and Events

From the outside, trade conferences can appear as the most boring events ever created. However, those who work them know that they're a gold mine for leads and generating business. A lot of networking happens at these conferences and it's in your best interest to show up at as many events as possible.

When searching for these events, don't restrict yourself to just trucking shows. Attend industry events, too. For instance, if you're a HAZMAT trucker, then attend a conference that is geared towards chemical manufacturers. You may not fully understand what's being discussed but that's not the point. You're there to connect with as many people as possible...so get connecting!

In the current environment, with COVID wrecking havoc globally, conferences have moved online, which isn't a great format no matter how you look at it. Thanks to more people preferring remote work, the future of most conferences seems to be online. Time will tell how this space will evolve.

For now, attending events is easy, since all you need is an internet connection and a device that can connect to it.

However, making connections with people is tough. There's no way of replicating the spontaneous human interactions that occur at an in-person event. Some conferences have virtual break rooms and business speed networking, where you talk to someone for a minute and move on, however, these formats don't capture the magic.

For now though, it's a good idea to take a look at the event attendee lists and see if you can network with people there. Connect with them on LinkedIn and prospect them to see if they have a need for your services. Remember, all of this is in conjunction with your other marketing activities. Don't lean on conferences all the time.

Trade shows are a good way to get the inside track on key people within industry alliances. Typically, these people tend to be higher-up in a company in the industry and knowing them is a good way to drum up business.

Don't forget the government in all of this. The government is one of the largest employers in the country and they always have a need for truckers. Connect with registered government contractors and you'll find them to be a steady source of loads. Remember that every other trucker out there is doing the same thing as you are, so you will have competition. However, once you layer this with your other activities, you'll manage to stand out.

This brings to an end our look at marketing methods. As you can see, they may be quite simple, but executing them is tough. What's more, you need to utilize them all together or else your efforts won't bear fruit. So be patient and build up to it. You want to get started on your marketing much before you buy your truck.

Ideally, you'll set up your business and a website, along with your LinkedIn profile, and start reaching out to people. Once you book hauls and receive firm indications that you'll have hauls, you can go all in on your business and either buy or lease yourself a rig. Getting into the marketing rhythm before hauling is a great way to hit the ground running. This way, you'll have a marketing machine working for you right from the start and you won't be sitting around waiting for loads to come to you. Plan everything in advance and you'll manage to achieve success from the beginning. Think of everything that could go wrong and develop strategies to mitigate these potential issues.

Lastly, try not to worry about all of this. Go ahead and make your moves! You have what it takes! You'll discover this once you begin doing it. Often, we scare ourselves by overthinking about the difficulty of our tasks. Simply set them aside and take the first step. You'll be just fine.

Creating Freight Lanes

One of the most important things you must do as an owner-operator is create a well-defined freight lane. It's one of the first questions that your prospective clients will ask you and you will need to have a good answer for them. A properly defined freight lane often seems like a risky thing to do at first.

After all, if you specified that you'll haul goods in just a few lanes, won't that diminish your ability to carry loads? For instance, if you define your lane from Des Moines, Iowa to Gary, Indiana, won't you miss out on loads that go to the Chicago area? Well, there is some truth to this but it likely won't play out the way you might think.

First, when designing your lane, you want to connect to an area that is bound to experience regular traffic. Ideally, both your starting and ending points will have regular traffic but make sure at least one is in high demand. That sounds like common sense but you'd be surprised at how many truckers drive between obscure places and expect business to come rushing to them. They end up switching lanes and driving as many as possible in a bid to drum up business.

So always design a lane that makes sense. Once you define your lane, stick to it! You'll come to be known as the person who drives a particular corridor and you'll gain a reputation. Once this happens, anyone who needs loads hauled in that corridor will come to you. If your local area doesn't have a single industry that makes sense, defining your corridor will help you stand out from the competition.

What's more, you'll be able to haul more LTL freight which will increase your earnings. There are many advantages to driving a fixed lane. Let's look at some of them.

Advantages

The biggest advantage of having a well-defined lane is that you'll have constant freight from the shippers who need goods hauled in that lane. What's more, you'll also come into contact with the relevant freight brokers and smaller shippers who need freight delivered in that route. This means you can build better relationships with these people and also minimize costs en route.

You do this by getting to know the best truck stops and the hidden routes that exist everywhere. Specialization is what gets you paid in trucking, so dive deep into a route and you'll end up making more money. If you run into trouble on the road, you'll know which repair facilities are the best and you can establish working relationships with them.

By giving them regular business, you can negotiate discounted rates for future trips, which will save you a lot of money. Driving a specialized lane will also give you more control over your revenue since you'll know exactly what the costs are and how much margin you need to add on top of it. Your world of unknowns will decrease dramatically and you're unlikely to be surprised by anything.

This is something that most unspecialized truckers miss. The better you know your lane, the better you'll plan your journeys and the lower your costs will be. You'll know when traffic is bad and what the best times are to drive. The result is less fatigue, better service, and more money. The best part is that if you specialize in a lane deeply enough, you'll be able to quote the cheapest rates and gain the lion's share of business that happens through it.

As you can see, there are qualitative and quantitative advantages to creating a highly specialized lane. Admittedly, it's true that you'll have to say no to potentially lucrative loads in different lanes. However, in trucking it's best to do narrow and deep rather than wide and shallow.

What I'm saying is that it's better to specialize in a single area and dominate this area instead of trying to do everything at once. This doesn't mean you should have just one lane. However, don't drive too many of them since this adds to your costs. Have a specialty and stick to it. Much like the hauls you carry, you need to understand the intricacies of the route you're servicing. This way, you'll end up creating massive advantages in your business that your competitors will find hard to overcome.

In the beginning, it'll seem as if specializing in one lane is a bad choice. However, be patient and invest in growing your expertise. An important caveat to mention here is you must pick a lane that is profitable to begin with. Pick a wrong lane and no amount of specialization or waiting is going to work for you. So do your research thoroughly and choose your lane wisely.

Over time, you'll find that business will become steady. At that point, you'll need to grow your client base to bring in more money and scale your operations.

Growing Your Client Base

Every business needs to grow in order to thrive in the long term. Many owner-operators start off strong but then end up moving backwards because they fail to grow their business. Conditions change all of the time, so you must always be pursuing growth. I'm not saying you need to become the biggest trucking operation in the world.

But you do need to have as many clients as possible in your pipeline. You never know when a load might fail to come through or some client's needs might change. If you don't have a wide client base, you're not going to have steady cash flow. This is why continuing to market yourself and putting effort into growing your client base is necessary.

As a rule of thumb, you want to work with at least five sources of work. These five sources could be direct shippers, freight brokers, or even a load board. The greater the number of direct shippers you have, the more you'll get paid every month. Thus, growing your client base isn't just about quantity, it's about increasing the quality of your clients, too.

In the beginning, you might be reliant on load boards, good freight brokers or a single direct client. Work to bring as many direct clients on board as possible and you'll manage to work less hours for more pay. It is a process, so don't expect things to change overnight. Be patient and keep taking action with respect to your marketing tasks.

Don't get too caught up with the five sources number. This is a rule of thumb. Some experienced owner-operators work with two clients and earn enough money. Some work with ten clients because they prefer greater volumes. You'll eventually find what's right for you and will land on a sweet spot.

Another rule of thumb is to never have a single client account for more than 20% of your income. That makes you fully dependent on them and in the case they change their terms, you're going to have a tough time compensating for their absence. Growing your client base and increasing their quality is simply a question of continuing to do the things that you've already learned about in this chapter.

These are a few additional tips.

Establish an Online Presence

In the long run, you always want to have an online presence. There are some successful owner-operators that have zero web presence but manage to land steady loads. Some newbies look at truckers like them and think a website or social media account isn't necessary. This is categorically false. You have to be present online and without it, you're dead in the water.

When starting out, you can get away with not having a website or social media account but it's a bit risky. At the very least, you need to have a LinkedIn profile up. Facebook doesn't let you have more than one account, so you can't create a separate one unless you create a business account.

There are many groups on Facebook dedicated to trucking and a business account isn't really necessary. It's better to focus on LinkedIn and network that way. Use Facebook with your personal profile and you'll be fine. Eventually, you want to get your website up and start publishing some content.

What kind of content? Well, it could be anything, such as maintenance tips for new operators, recording your loads (with sensitive information removed), and so on. Don't overthink this. A well-maintained website conveys professionalism and activity. A prospective client isn't going to read your blog posts for tips, but they'll know you're active and are looking for work. Besides, a good website conveys authority and you'll come across as a professional instead of a bum with a truck.

Helping out other truckers is a good way of building your credibility. You can help new truckers and help in answering their questions. By doing this, you'll come to be viewed as someone who has authority, even if you aren't the most experienced owner-operator out there. Mind you, don't talk about things you know nothing about, you'll be unmasked soon. Instead, look to help people and discuss events native to your lane and you'll be fine.

You can even segment your subscribers and send multiple newsletters. For instance, you can send a newsletter to prospective clients and send another "helpful tips" newsletter to the beginner truckers. If all this sounds complex, then stick to a single prospect newsletter. At the end of the day, it's all about helping clients get to know you better, so don't sweat it too much.

Keep putting consistent effort and you'll see results.

Paid Ads

Paid ads tend to occupy the forefront of any discussion when it comes to marketing. However, they're pretty inefficient and you need a full time staff member looking after your expenses. Online ad platforms are designed to help you optimize how much money you spend. You can spend very little and gain exposure.

However, the opposite is the typical experience. There's so much competition these days that your ad budgets will slowly expand. Also remember that companies like Facebook and Google earn money by charging you money for ads. They're not in business to give you exposure. Their ad platforms are almost purposefully byzantine and designed to get you to spend as much cash as possible.

For these reasons, digital advertising can go horribly wrong. It's best to hire an ads expert if you choose to go down this route, or even consider hiring an agency. This costs money, as you can imagine. It's best to invest in expertise. You might be tempted to DIY this after reading some 10,000 word guide to paid ads online.

However, this isn't your area of expertise. You're great at hauling loads and pleasing customers with your service and efficiency. Running ads and managing ad budgets isn't your thing. Stay in your lane at all times and hire out everything else. This is how you'll grow your business efficiently.

If you don't have the budget to hire someone or run ads, then don't do it. It's not necessary to spend a ton of money on paid ads to be successful. Networking and generating organic traffic the way I've shown you are the best strategies. Don't become a big tech donor for no reason.

Reviews

Customers these days place huge importance on the reviews a business receives. Make it a habit to ask for testimonials and reviews once you've finished hauling a load. Most owner-operators don't do this and think their customers will leave a review automatically. Some are simply too shy to ask for a review.

The first step is to register your business with Google and make sure it shows up on Google Maps. Without this, your customers cannot leave you a review. The way to set up a pin on Google Maps is easy. Simply login using your business' email address (or any email connected to your business) and enter the location.

Once your pin is up, you'll receive a link to your business listing and can send this to your clients and ask them to leave a positive review. Make sure you ask them if they were satisfied with your service. If they hint at something unsatisfactory, don't send them your link. It's best to ask them upfront, in-person for a review. Tell them you'll send them a link to leave a review via email and would they mind leaving a favorable review.

Respond to their review with a note of thanks since this makes you seem like a real person and not a corporate suit. Interaction with your customers makes your reviews seem more legitimate and you'll come across as someone who cares about the service they provide.

Other sites such as Yelp or even customer testimonials on your LinkedIn profile and website are extremely important. Collect them from customers and highlight them. These reviews are what people use to make buying decisions so make it easy for them to get in touch with you.

Chapter 4:

Back-End Operations

Running a business is a tough task and at times, it will feel like there's simply too as if there's too much to do. Don't freak out when this happens, it's a normal thing to experience. Most new business owners experience such hiccups and the key to solving them is to create processes that make your life easier.

The thing to remember is that you have three priorities that are central to your business. The first is on-time deliveries. This is the most important thing for your business because nothing matters to the client more than receiving their loads on time. Deliver it late or don't communicate well with your clients regarding delays and you're not going to bring in a lot of business. So prioritize this at all times!

The second most important priority is to ensure your deliveries are safe and secure. Safety extends beyond the way your load is secured. It also has to do with the way you conduct yourself when you drive. If you don't take care of yourself and make sure you're well rested before driving, you're not going to deliver your loads on time. You'll also make mistakes and ruin your reputation.

As I said previously, clients care about your safety record and compliance since it's a reflection of your professionalism. Think of it this way: If you were looking to hire a plumber, would you hire someone who has a reputation of injuring themselves in the workplace, irrespective of how well they did their job? The liability alone makes them a bad hire. So always be compliant with regulations and convey your commitment to the rules to your customer.

Lastly, prices are important. This doesn't mean every client is looking for bargain basement prices. However, your prices must be reasonable. The ideal price is one where everyone wins. The client receives a good deal and you are compensated adequately, as well.

Before diving into the rest of this chapter, make a note of these priorities and points. Without them, you won't have a business, so always orient everything to ensure these goals are fulfilled.

People

To grow your business efficiently, you're going to need to work with and hire people. There's no way around it. You might see the word "people" and think you will need to spend a great deal of money. It's important to realize that it's possible to grow your business without hiring a lot of employees. I know many owner-operators who run successful operations and outsource or hire out the majority of their back office tasks, and even their marketing.

All of the roles I'll highlight here can be outsourced. Additionally, you won't need some of these rules until you reach a certain size. So don't think you have to rush out and hire for all of these roles. Take it slow and plan your business' growth step by step.

Office Manager

Once you start hauling enough loads, you're going to start accumulating paperwork. You'll need to digitize these records for audit purposes and can't leave them sitting around in a bunch of paper files. Some documents will have to be preserved in their original format and you'll need secure storage for them.

The long and short of it is: You need an office manager or a filing system that you can easily use to retrieve records. Hiring a person to do this task is tough at first since you'll probably not be making enough money to pay them a decent salary. There are solutions though!

First off, create online file keeping systems in the cloud. This is as simple as signing up for a Dropbox or Google Drive account and storing all documents there. Once you sign something, scan it and upload it. You can now access this document anywhere, as long as there's an internet connection.

At some point, you'll begin receiving too many requests from clients to respond to while on the road. If you can't find someone to handle them cheaply, the best thing to do is to visit a freelancer website like Upwork and hire a Virtual Assistant (VA). These freelancers are based all around the world and you can hire someone cheaply to execute basic file maintenance tasks. You can't outsource everything since you can't send them paper copies. However, responding to emails and social media is easy through the Virtual Assistant route. Make sure you evaluate them for exceptional spoken and written skills as they will be representing your business.

If you want something closer to home, try hiring a local college student as an intern. They're always looking to make more money and you can outsource a greater number of tasks to them. Make sure you enforce strict working hours, even if it's remote, and you'll be fine.

Once you're making enough to pay someone full time, hire an employee or continue with this model, whatever fits you. Some truckers use their partners' help with managing paperwork so if that's an option, it's a good one for you.

Sales Staff

Initially, you'll have to handle all sales-related tasks yourself as I've described in the previous chapter. However, once you get to a certain size, it's better to hire a salesperson who can handle client requests and reach out to prospective clients. Usually, when you're hauling for five clients or more, it helps to have a salesperson on staff.

You'll need a team if your plan is to grow your business to a point where you want to hire other truckers to drive for you. Some owner-operators go down this route and eventually give up driving to run their business from their home base. If this appeals to you, you'll need to invest in hiring a sales staff and incentivizing them to bring you work.

Don't rush into hiring a sales staff. Take your time with it and grow slowly. Remember that a sales staff isn't a magic bullet that will automatically bring a bunch of clients to you. Marketing staff tend to get grouped together with sales. The only exception is if you're running paid ads and are commissioning content on a regular basis for your website and social media channels.

In that case, you'll need a marketing department to handle all of this. In the beginning, it's best to combine the sales and marketing roles and split them gradually as you grow.

Bookkeeper

This role is extremely important, and it's one that you should have right from the start. Bookkeeping is something many owners underrate, so I encourage you not to make this mistake. At the very least, you should have someone recording receipts and maintaining a log of expenses and incoming cash. You can do this yourself, of course.

Make sure you create a robust spreadsheet and record all of your expenses and revenue regularly. At the end of the year, you'll need to file your taxes with the government, so you'll have to hire an accountant to do this for you. Needless to say, you should hire someone who is qualified and has experience. Check with your network to get in touch with such individuals.

You don't have to hire a full-time accountant for your staff until you're receiving multiple load requests daily and have to process invoices every other day. Until you reach this stage, contracting an accountant is fine.

Dispatcher

Do you recall me saying that dispatchers could help you to get customers? Well, once you receive enough loads to hire other trucks, you need a dispatcher. In the beginning, you can contract an agency to handle this for you. They'll usually provide other back office-related services, as well. However, if you're hauling multiple loads daily (as a company), it's best to hire a dispatcher.

Some companies combine the roles of office manager and dispatcher. It depends on the volume of loads you receive. Don't sweat it too much though. You'll figure it out once you get the loads and client requests coming in.

Note that you'll be doing all of these tasks, except accounting, yourself at first, so it will be hectic. Speak to people in your network to figure out the best ways of getting these tasks done and you'll manage to transition from a solo entrepreneur to a medium sized business effortlessly.

How to Hire

Your business is only as good as the people you hire. It sounds cliche but it's true. At first, you'll struggle to attract the best candidates since most people look for security when applying for a job. Once you hire someone and decide to terminate them, you may find that getting rid of them isn't easy either. Bad employees are notorious for sticking to your business for much longer than comfortable.

This means you need to plan your hiring in advance and carefully. Advertise on local job boards and college campuses and lean on your network to find people who are qualified. Don't ever be in a rush to hire someone and take your time vetting their qualifications. Create detailed job descriptions that clearly identify the expected responsibilities and tasks. That way there's no misunderstanding possible.

Once you hire someone, make sure you train them well. Many owners forget that the tasks they've been executing aren't obvious to everyone. You must trust your new hires to do the job you've hired them for and allow them space to make mistakes. It's how they'll learn. Don't expect them to start functioning at a high level immediately.

Record Keeping

Every business needs to maintain accurate records and yours is no different. It's a good idea to maintain accurate records right from the beginning so that you won't have to scramble at the last minute to get everything straight. Aside from your receipts and load documents, you need to maintain compliance-related documents as well. Here they are in no particular order.

Qualification Files and Employee Records

You should always have copies of your CDL handy and store the originals in your office or a safe location. Needless to say, you should carry your CDL with you at all times. If you're hiring other truckers, you need to make sure you have all of their records on file too.

If you've hired employees, you will need to save all of their important information such as their social security numbers and other personal details. This information has to be secured at all times and you must have a robust record-keeping system. Lose this information and you'll risk being held liable for disclosing personal information.

Logs

Your logs are more than just paperwork. They're proof of how well you've driven and your experience as a driver. If you've hired other truckers to work for you, you need to have copies of their logs on file as well. These days, driver logs are electronic so record keeping is fairly straightforward. However, you should store them in a safe place and organize them appropriately.

The reason you need to store logs comes down to liability. If there's an accident or a dispute of some kind, the first documents to be checked are the logs. So make sure they're well stored.

HOS Records

Your driver log is a record of how safely you've driven. However, from a compliance standpoint, your Hours of Service or (HOS) logs are more important since they record how well you've complied with regulations. HOS logs are monitored and created via your ELD or electronic logging device. This is connected to your truck and tracks all the relevant status and the time you've spent in them.

Make sure to backup all of your HOS records in a secure place. If your ELD is damaged or corrupted, or if your primary storage source is corrupted, backups come in handy.

Accident Reports

No one wants to be part of an accident but if something like this does happen, you should maintain meticulous records.

Document everything and store these files even if you were the one at fault. You don't have to go to the extent of taking detailed pictures and videos but it can't hurt.

A mistake that some owner-operators make is to think that minor accidents don't count for much. Remember to document everything and follow all lawful procedures when you run into trouble.

DVIR

DVIR stands for driver vehicle inspection report and this is a pre-trip inspection that you must complete according to Federal guidelines. The penalties for not completing a DVIR according to procedures are massive, so you must never risk this. If a safety non-compliance fine hits your record, you can wave goodbye to top-tier clients.

Many owner-operators have trouble conducting the inspection according to guidelines. It's a good idea to download an app such as *KeepTrucking* that simplifies the DVIR process. You can follow the on-screen prompts and record everything that happens. You should begin with recording and addressing the defects from the previous DVIR, which you'll complete at the end of the trip, and sign off on those.

You should never drive your truck with open issues on the previous DVIR. Some truckers take a risk but as an owner-operator, you should never do this. There's too much at stake. Make sure you store your DVIRs for at least three months after completion since this is Federal law.

IFTA Returns

IFTA stands for international fuel tax agreement and it simplifies your fuel tax filings. As a commercial vehicle that drives through multiple states, your truck consumes fuel in all of them and thus, each state will want its own cut of the fuel tax you pay. IFTA simplifies this by allowing you to file only one tax return every quarter. Ensure that your IFTA decal is prominently displayed when your truck is operating and make sure your ELD is recording everything relevant to simplify and automate your record keeping.

Maintenance Records

Closely tied to your DVIRs are your maintenance records. Make sure you tie the DVIRs to the maintenance records when applicable. Needless to say, record all maintenance actions you take. If you've conducted some DIY maintenance, then record it with photos or videos. You'll need these records when selling your truck or trading it in to show you've taken good care of it.

Drug and Alcohol Testing Results

The government takes drug and alcohol testing seriously and the last thing you want is to get pulled over for a DUI. You'll have to get tested for policy violations at certain periods throughout the year depending on the company you're driving for. Typically, owner-operators must register at a local consortium and everyone in that group is tested at the same time.

You can check at the local DOT office to inquire about the procedures you need to follow to apply to a consortium.

These are the primary documents you need to keep records of in most situations. As a rule of thumb, don't throw anything away unless it's over ten years old. Again, use your common sense. Digitize everything so that you're not storing everything on paper. You'll avoid clutter and you won't risk having documents damaged.

Have a meticulous record keeping process and always prioritize storing your documents and logs. Many owner-operators get themselves into trouble because they allow a backlog to build up with regards to compliance. Don't be this person. Always maintain meticulous records and you'll be just fine.

Labeling receipts and sorting all of your documents is a good practice to follow. Remember that while all of this is tedious, it helps you achieve the primary goals addressed in the beginning of this chapter.

Taxes

No one can avoid taxes completely, so without further ado, let's get into it! A lot of tax filings will be taken care of by your accountant. However, it's helpful to understand the process. Experienced owners take care of tax filing by themselves, provided there aren't any complications. When starting out, I don't recommend doing this since it might lead to complications. There are two broad categories of taxes you'll be liable to pay.

The first are self-employment taxes and the second are state and federal taxes. The process is quite straightforward.

Determining Taxes

Bookkeeping is the bedrock of solid tax preparation. To this end, you must maintain a reliable record of expenses and revenue. Subtract your expenses from revenue and you'll arrive at your yearly income. It's helpful to do this every month and at the end of the year, you can simply add the monthly figures. Remember that expenses should be recorded the month that you paid them.

All of these figures need to be reported to the IRS and you'll do this via Schedule C (Form 1040). Note that this form applies only if you're a sole proprietor. LLCs and companies have separate filing requirements and tend to be more complex. Consult a qualified CPA to prepare your taxes if you're not a sole-proprietor.

The results of Schedule C have to be transferred to the main Form 1040. The form is self-explanatory and the IRS provides detailed guidelines concerning filling the form. Once you're done, you need to fill out Schedule SE which gives you the amount of self-employment taxes you owe.

This amount is over and above any amount you owe or are owed from the Form 1040 filing. You can mail your returns to the IRS with your check or file them electronically on the IRS website. You can pay by credit or debit card online.

Deductions

Every business owner loves deductions but you must be careful. Claim too many deductions and you'll have the IRS auditing you for discrepancies. It's important to realize that you cannot claim everything as a deduction. The biggest deduction you can claim are meals away from home. These are considered business expenses and can be claimed. Just make sure you preserve all receipts and digitize them as quickly as possible.

Note that you can't claim the entire expense. The IRS allows for a deduction of $63 per day and 80% of this amount is deductible.

Next we have lodging, which is fully deductible. However, there are some caveats. You need to have a physical home address. If the IRS comes knocking, you should have your lease, mortgage deed or utility bills, on hand to prove you're a resident at that address. As long as you satisfy this requirement, you can claim lodging expenses. Make sure you save your receipts.

There are additional "on the road" expenses you can claim as well. These expenses must be necessary for you to complete your job. For instance, laundry expenses are deductible since they're considered necessary. Other examples include safety gear, CB radios, GPS devices and maps.

The IRS doesn't need receipts for expenses under $75. However, it's best to be safe and store all receipts in case you get audited. You can sneak in a few unauthorized expenses this way but don't get carried away. An audit is not a good experience and you might end up paying much more than you intended.

One of the more complicated deductions you can claim are vehicle cost write-offs. A write-off is, in accounting terms, a loss. The company simply eats it all in one go so that it doesn't depress earnings in the long run. As an owner-operator, you have three choices: The first is to write off up to $510,000 in the year your vehicle is put into service. Essentially, you write off the cost of your truck in one shot.

The second is to write off 50% of the cost of the truck in the first year followed by normal depreciation, which is typically 10%. Lastly, you can assume normal depreciation and write off your truck over time.

All of these choices have tax implications. Write off the cost of your truck in the first year and you're going to have a loss on your books. Thus, you won't owe taxes, unless you manage to earn more than $510,000, which I'm going to say is a bit far-fetched. However, you won't be able to claim this deduction again until you buy a new truck. This means your second, third and subsequent year taxes will be higher than with the other options.

The 50% depreciation write-off will likely have you paying no taxes, depending on how much work you source and the cost of your truck. If you purchase a truck for $50,000, you can write off $25,000. If you make more than this, which you probably will, you'll owe taxes on profits. However, in subsequent years, your tax bill will be greater because you'll end up writing off your truck in a shorter period of time. You'll have just 50% of the truck's value to depreciate on your books, after all.

The last option is the conventional one where you'll slowly depreciate the value of your truck. It leads to a steady write-off over time and a sustained tax deduction. If your business is successful, you'll find that this option will be the most profitable. The sustained depreciation will reduce your tax bill as your income increases over the years. The other methods won't have you taking deductions, so you'll end up paying more taxes. Ultimately, it's best to speak to your accountant to figure out what will work the best for you

Note that if you're leasing your truck, you can't deduct anything except your lease payments since you don't own your truck.

Hopefully now you can see why leasing isn't always the best option.

You can claim general business expenses as deductions, too. Cleaning expenses, association dues, office supplies, DOT physicals, and so on, can be deducted as they are a part of keeping your business going.

Tips

If you're an LLC or a corporation, your accountant will file taxes monthly for you. This is because the taxes you owe can add up quickly and it's easier to file a monthly amount with the IRS and then calculate the excess or deficit at the end of the year and claim it. Sole proprietors can do this as well but it's best to consult your accountant. The best way to avoid audits and other legal hassles is to be honest. The second best way is to prove your honesty by keeping meticulous records. Always log your receipts and digitize them by taking a photo and uploading it to the cloud (your online storage service).

Log everything that you do and keep as much proof as possible. Think of it this way: If someone wants to examine your business, you'll be able to throw enough paper at them to drown them. The cost of filing taxes isn't very high but some owners want to save this money and end up doing everything themselves.

If you're experienced enough, it's worth doing it this way. If you're not, there are specialists out there who can do it for you much quicker. The time it takes you to prepare your taxes by yourself could be spent hauling. It's best to hire out this job to a CPA and use your time efficiently. Besides, a good CPA will save you money in the long run by highlighting deductions and credits you can apply for.

One of the best ways of minimizing your tax bill is to set up a retirement account, like an IRA or 401(k) and contribute pre-tax dollars to it. This money will be taxed only once if you withdraw it at the age of 59 ½ and until then, you can keep contributing. There are contribution limits, so it's not as if you can keep pushing unlimited sums of cash in there. However, you should contribute the maximum allowed limit to save tax dollars.

Something else to consider is tracked personal vehicle miles. You'll be using your personal vehicle to run business-related errands such as going shopping for parts, visiting the bank, meeting a client, and so on. You can claim these miles as deductions despite not using your truck. So be sure to keep a track of them at all times.

Handling Renewals

Renewals don't take much time but the penalties for forgetting to renew your paperwork can be costly. The best way to avoid these needless penalties is to get organized and keep good records. Set alarm reminders on your phone and computer so that you're reminded when the time comes to renew your paperwork.

Your authority is the primary document that needs renewal, along with your CDL. The renewal processes for both are quite straightforward. I'll cover them in more detail in the next chapter but for now, just understand that you'll have to pay the fees and that's pretty much it. Your IRP plates and IFTA decal has to be renewed as well.

Each of these renewals have slightly different procedures, even if they're simple. It's best to maintain a spreadsheet that outlines all the processes so that you can refer to it and make sure all renewals go through seamlessly.

Making sure you renew your paperwork on time is just a matter of keeping good records and not losing track of your documents. Create sound processes and the rest will fall into place

Time Management

As a business owner, your time is going to be stretched thin. At first, it's going to be overwhelming since you'll feel as if you need to perform surgery while driving your rig. Don't worry, you'll adjust to the demands on your time eventually. As I've mentioned before, plan your tasks in advance as much as possible and be ready for any last-minute demands. Accept that it will be challenging and you'll manage to handle your tasks better.

Developing good time management habits is helpful as well. A lot of these tips will become obvious as you grow along your journey as an owner-operator. However, it's best to take note of them for now and start developing them immediately.

Avoid Multitasking

Here's a news flash: There's no such thing as multitasking. There's focusing on what's in front of you and there's doing a bad job of focusing. Always focus on what's in front of you and don't do two things at once. You hear many corporate types boast about multitasking. Well, some may say that they have the attention span of a goldfish. So don't think you're missing out on anything!

A close cousin of multitasking is procrastination. While multitaskers try to do everything at once, procrastinators keep pushing things down the road. They don't seem close cousins at first but I believe both behaviors occur because of an underlying fear or anxiety about the tasks at hand.

At first, the mountain of tasks in front of you will seem overwhelming and you might either try to get all of it out of the way or try to avoid doing it. The root cause is a lack of organization. Build good habits from the beginning by maintaining spreadsheets and creating task lists for yourself.

Organization is a habit and it takes time to build. Keep doing it everyday and you'll soon manage to execute your tasks effortlessly. Make sure that the lists you create are realistic. Often, people create unrealistic lists and use that as an excuse to put things off. Make sure you're not doing this inadvertently.

Schedule Email and Communication

Email tends to disrupt everyone's work days. The best way to handle it is to schedule a time during which you'll respond to communications and not stray from that schedule. Usually, it's best to answer emails during your breaks, five minutes at a time. Don't use your entire break to answer emails since this defeats the purpose.

The same advice applies to answering phone calls. Let people leave you a message and call them back when you're free. While you want to answer people promptly, you don't want to drop everything to answer their call. After all, you'll be hauling loads during the day and can't be on your phone all the time.

Prioritize your break times so that you truly look forward to them. Don't simply sit around doing nothing. Relax completely and do something that rests your mind. Walking along a trail might boost your energy levels or simply sipping coffee might do the trick. Whatever energizes you, make sure you do it and prioritize it.

Often, unplanned situations will arise. Do your best and deal with them as they arise. Don't panic and do something in haste. That's the easiest way to make the problem worse. Take your time with it and work on the issue.

Technology Aids

Once you scale your business to a point where you'll hire other drivers, you'll find that technology will come to your aid when it comes to productivity and compliance. Scaling a company is tough since you'll have to rely on processes and other people to get things done. You won't be able to do everything yourself as there simply won't be enough time.

One piece of technology that every rig driver must have, irrespective of the size of their company, is a dashcam. They are lifesavers and will keep you safe from a variety of scams out there. Many scam artists take advantage of rig drivers by braking heavily in front of the rig so as to cause a collision or drive in front of the rig and brake-check them.

Without a dashcam, the driver who rear-ended the vehicle in front is usually found at fault. Dashcams can prove your innocence. They're also handy in proving your innocence in other accidents and the police use them to record proof in these cases. If you're hiring other truckers, then equipping their trucks with dashcams is a no-brainer. It helps you keep track of their driving and indemnifies you in case of accidents.

Use driver scorecards to evaluate your workforce. Track metrics such as miles per gallon, delivery punctuality, and compliance. Poor drivers will hurt your business very quickly, so you will want to track their behavior in your trucks at all times. I'm not saying you should have a video camera recording them. you need to make sure they're driving safely and are compliant with laws at all times.

Tools, such as real time GPS tracking, geo fencing, and facility insight reports, will help you understand what your business is doing well and where you need to improve. Installing a TMS (transportation management software) or truck scheduling software will help you create dynamic schedules that help you bring the best out of your drivers without overloading them with too much work.

Chapter 5:

Safety and Compliance

Compliance and safety are extremely important when operating a trucking business. The government takes both of them very seriously and you should never risk compromising on these regulations. As a truck owner, it's your responsibility to understand these regulations. You can't use ignorance as an excuse, so make sure you're always up to speed with them.

Violating these rules costs a lot of money. In extreme cases, the Department of Transportation will order the closure of your business. FMCSA or the Federal Motor Carrier Safety Administration is the primary regulatory body that you'll have to pay attention to. Your authority and permits will be granted by them.

Violating FMCSA guidelines results in fines ranging from $300 to $191,000. Your CDL will be suspended and if you operate your business during this time, another fine of $24,000 will be levied. In short, you want to take them seriously and not flout the rules.

Aside from FMCSA, the Department of Transportation (DOT) also conducts a wide variety of checks. Many of these inspections are random and usually occur at rest stops. It isn't unusual to stop and have a DOT inspector select your truck for random inspection. Typically, they'll want to check your ELD for status history and your DVIRs. They might pull you over for a detailed inspection but it's rare.

In addition to random checks, you'll need to submit your truck for full inspection. Inspectors, typically former truckers themselves, will scrutinize your truck for safety and you need to make sure all problems are taken care of.

All of this might sound a bit draconian on paper. However, following the rules and regulations is actually quite straightforward. They help keep you safe and ensure that road safety isn't compromised.

Regulations

What are the most important regulations that you must be aware of? The primary regulations deal with HOS, DVIRs, and driver qualifications. Let's look at them closely.

Hours of Service

HOS or Hours of Service is the most important regulation you need to be aware of. These rules specify how long you can drive your truck on the road and how often you need to take rest breaks. Most driver accidents are caused by fatigue, so following HOS regulations is important for your sake.

The rules are fairly straightforward but it can be confusing for new truckers. Here are the important highlights. Within a 14 hour period, truckers can drive for no more than 11 consecutive hours. What this rule says is you have 14 hours of driving time and you can break your driving shifts up as you please. However, you cannot drive for more than 11 hours at once. Once this 14 hour driving period finishes, you must rest for 10 consecutive hours.

If truckers have driven for 14 consecutive hours, they must go off duty on the 15th hour, for at least 10 consecutive hours. In addition to this, no trucker can drive for more than 60 hours over seven consecutive days or 70 hours over eight consecutive days. Once this limit is reached, the trucker must take 34 consecutive hours off duty.

Finally, after driving for eight hours, truckers must take a 30 minute break. The status on your ELD doesn't have to be flipped to off-duty. You can be on-duty but you must not drive.

All of these rules put together seem complicated and it can get confusing fast. Here's a simple rule of thumb. Don't drive for more than 14 hours per day. Drive for a maximum of 11 hours consecutively. Rest as much as you can and start driving the next day. Make sure you flip your ELD into the appropriate statuses since this will help you figure out how much you need to rest and how much you can drive.

To further simplify things, you can download an HOS compliance app on your phone and track your hours there. The app crunches all the numbers for you and tells you when you can drive and for how long. Note that in emergency or adverse weather conditions, HOS rules can be suspended.

DVIR

Driver vehicle inspection reports are the next big compliance item on the list. FMCSA publishes a DVIR template report. Download this and walk through the list, recording all the necessary observations. Typically, these involve checking your tires, brakes, lights, and other load restraining equipment.

You'll need to complete them twice everyday. First before you begin driving and second when you finish driving. Any issues that you find have to be addressed as quickly as possible. Make sure your DVIRs are stored for a period of three months, at a minimum. It's best to digitize your DVIRs and store them immediately.

If you encounter a surprise inspection one of the first things an inspector will ask you for is your DVIR. So make sure you have them handy and don't try to shortcut your inspections. Note that you'll have to document all repairs you've made as well.

IFTA

IFTA simplifies your fuel tax filings but it requires you to keep meticulous records of where you've been and the number of miles you drove in each state. Typically, your ELD will have functionality that will help you keep track of everything. However, you should always double check to make sure everything is being tracked.

Make sure your ELD is tracking your odometer and your location at all times and your IFTA filings become simple.

Driver Qualification File

This file should be stored in your office or place of business. If you're a sole proprietor, you don't have to worry about this too much. However, if you've hired drivers then you have to maintain this file meticulously. FMCSA requires this file to be maintained for at least three years and for every driver you've hired.

For starters, the file has to have the driver's application for employment, fully completed and signed. All drivers must list employers they've worked for in the last 10 years. In addition to the employment history, you must also document driver safety history and whether any violations of drug and alcohol regulations occurred.

Typically, these records must be collected from previous employers and all requests for these documents must be maintained. If the driver was involved in an accident or any safety violation, then the investigation process, the outcome, and the driver's actions during that time must also be recorded on their file.

A copy of the driver's motor vehicle record which you'll have to obtain from the DMV must also be on file. This MVR must be updated annually and the latest copies must be on file, for as long as the driver is employed with your company. In addition to this, companies must also file their driver's certification of violations.

This is a list of driving violations that the driver has been a part of over the past year. The law states that the certification of violations must be compared to the MVR to assess a driver's safety record. The driver's road test or equivalent test result must be on file as well, along with a copy of their CDL.

Every driver must pass a medical examination and employers must file the medical examiner's certificate. This certificate must be renewed every two years, unless the examiner specifies a different date. Drivers with medical impairments must obtain a Skill Performance Evaluation Certificate and their employers must have a copy of this on file.

Lastly, employers must have copies of their drivers' previous drug and alcohol testing results. If an employee refuses to make these records available, they cannot operate a commercial motor vehicle.

Other Regulations

While the above points are the major regulations you have to follow, there are smaller ones too. If you're hiring truckers then you need to conduct regular drug and alcohol tests and store those results in their driver files. In addition, you're responsible for ensuring your drivers follow the regulations as stated.

Make sure all of your trucks have ELDs installed since this is a Congressional mandate. If you've been driving for over 10 years, you might remember the era of pen and paper, but those days are long gone.

Another regulation that drivers must be aware of is idling time limits. Pollution concerns mean that some states limit the amount of time truck engines can idle. Your ELD captures this information so it's not as if you'll be pulled up for exceeding limits immediately. DOT inspectors check for these violations so it's best to understand idling limits before you transit through a state.

Similarly, weight limits are enforced as well. Each state has different limits and you should always haul loads below the limit. The fines are usually north of $25,000 so you'll face hefty penalties for non-compliance.

DOT Compliance Checklist

All of these regulations might cause your head to spin. Helpfully, the DOT publishes a checklist you can use to ensure you're always compliant. Typically, DOT inspectors work through these checklists when auditing you for compliance. Here are the important points in this list:

1. CDL List - Have a copy of FMCSA rules in your office. Every driver should receive a copy and must sign it and hand it back to you, while retaining a copy. All DVIRs and driver HOS logs must be filed. All vehicles must be marked with their DOT number and you must create a maintenance program.

2. Drug and Alcohol Compliance - All drivers must have a copy of the DOT's policies. Companies must file drivers' pre-employment drug tests. At least 50% of your drivers must be randomly tested for drug abuse every year. 10% of your drivers must be randomly tested for alcohol abuse each year. Ensure that all supervisors have completed the DOT training program.

As you can see, these two points are a collection of everything you've already read about. Follow the rules and you'll be just fine. Note that a lot of these checklists apply to large trucking companies. As a solo owner-operator, you need to keep copies of all tests, HOS logs, and DVIRs, and will have to sign up to a drug testing consortium. Other than that, you don't have much to worry about from a compliance perspective.

CSA and BASICs

CSA stands for Compliance, Safety, and Accountability and it's something every trucker needs to worry about. Your CSA score directly impacts your ability to work and the judging process isn't always fair to those who have unexpected incidents.

However, the system works at a high level and accounts for a wide range of circumstances.

Closely related to the CSA categories are FMCSA's Behavior Analysis and Safety Improvement Categories (BASICs). Together, these two evaluation criteria give you a driver score that reflects how well you manage to operate your truck. There are seven categories you'll be evaluated on:

1. Unsafe driving
2. Crash indicator
3. HOS compliance
4. DVIR logs and vehicle maintenance
5. Drug and alcohol compliance records
6. HAZMAT compliance (if you haul these loads)
7. Driver fitness (any debilitating physical injuries or issues)

Monitoring your scores is the best way to make sure you don't suffer in the long run. Think of these scores as your credit score. You don't have to check-in on them all the time but you should be aware of where you roughly land. Follow the rules and always remain compliant. The scores will take care of themselves.

A good way of avoiding any major issues with maintenance or safety-related breakdowns is to install sensors on sensitive portions of your truck. This especially applies to areas like your engine and transmission. All trucks come equipped with sensors anyway but some older models might lack these features. Consider installing them so that you're alerted before a problem hits. That way you won't inadvertently lower your scores because of an incident.

Safety

Safety is all-important when you're driving. Not only are you responsible for your own safety, you have to make sure you don't jeopardize the safety of other drivers on the road. A big rig can cause significant damage if you lose control of it. Here are some important safety points to take care of whenever you hit the road.

Use Technology

ELDs, GPS systems, sensor systems, dash cams, and trailer trackers are just some examples of technology that keeps you safe. You need to have an ELD at all times since this is mandated by law. However, I consider dash cams just as important. You never know what sort of conditions you'll run into when driving and a dash cam can get you out of trouble quickly.

There's always new tech arriving on the market so make sure you speak to your network and stay up to date with developments.

Always Prepare

Once you begin driving a lane, you'll get to know its characteristics pretty well. If it's a short haul, then you're not going to have too many issues. However, long haul truckers are often hit with surprises along certain stretches since their routes are long and some parts can deteriorate. Before setting off on a haul, it's a good idea to keep your ears peeled for information of disruptions or other delays along your lane.

Speak to people who have recently driven that route for information and things to watch out for. Make sure you carry out basic maintenance and give your rig a thorough once-over before setting off. The last thing you want is under-inflated tires causing you to burn more fuel or get involved in an accident.

Always report what you find over the CB network. It's helpful to other truckers driving along that lane and you'll find more people reciprocating.

Watch Out for Weather

Freezing rain, tornados, thunderstorms, heat waves or strong winds, can cause nightmares in a hurry if you're a trucker. Don't even think about driving through such dangerous conditions. Remember that the contracts you sign have clauses in them that lets you off the hook in case of inclement or unforeseen weather. So don't think you have to drive through this weather to deliver your haul.

It's best to pull over to a rest stop or a safe shoulder and ride out the storm. Your equipment is precious so don't risk getting involved in an accident during such times.

Take Care of Personal Safety

Keeping your rig safe is one thing but many truckers neglect basic personal safety measures. Always be aware of your surroundings and secure your cab at all times. Be wary of people who could potentially damage your rig at rest stops and don't walk between trailers. Always ensure you're visible when walking outside your cab by wearing protective clothing and sticking to well lit areas.

To make your cab even safer, you can use velcro and bed sheets to cover the windows. Make sure you keep your phone, laptop, and GPS systems out of sight and securely locked away. Another tip is to run your seat belt straps through the door handles to prevent them from being opened from the outside.

Make sure you have basic repair tools along with bug spray and at least two flashlights. Carry spare batteries as well to account for emergencies. Carrying a padlock with you is also a good idea in case you need to secure your trailer. It's also a good idea to check-in with someone on the phone and let them know where you are if you're pulling into an unfamiliar area that doesn't look very secure.

Stay Healthy

You're of no use to anyone if you don't take care of your health. Remember to always stay hydrated and avoid drinking too many energy drinks. They usually lead to energy crashes and you'll be extremely fatigued. Instead, eat as many home cooked meals as possible and avoid eating junk food. Exercise as much as you can since this not only refreshes your body but your mind as well.

Stay on top of your vitamin supplements and get enough sunlight exposure. Taking care of yourself isn't rocket science. Just follow common sense techniques to make sure you aren't falling sick.

Prepare for Breakdowns

As much as you don't want it to happen, you're going to have a breakdown at some point. How you handle these situations will define your trucking experience since you never know what can go wrong. The most important thing in this situation is to know who to call. Always have a list of emergency numbers you can call to seek help.

When you're an owner-operator, you can't call your company's helpline and have them take care of everything. Instead, you should call your insurance provider or dealer to check whether there's anyone in the local area who can help you out. Alternatively, if you've driven that lane previously, you'll probably know who to call. Make sure you have your emergency list written down at all times. If your phone dies, you won't be able to seek help or access those numbers.

Remember to set out safety triangles and use reflective equipment to warn other motorists of a potential hazard.

Maintain Your Truck

Proactive maintenance will help you head off any major problems down the road. Check your oil and replace it when the manufacturer recommends it. Rotate your tires and always perform a visual check for exterior damage. Make sure your lights, mirrors, and brakes are in good order.

Make sure the mechanics you contract are ASE certified and are reliable. Keep your truck clean and polished at all times since this helps prevent rust. It's best to get your truck fixed at dealerships since they tend to have all tools needed to fix your issues.

Do Your Research

Rules and regulations change all the time and it's impossible for a book or a single person to help you stay up to date. FMCSA has detailed information on their website that you can refer to. Sure, a lot of it is legalese but pay attention to their news releases. They typically contain a load of useful information and will help you understand any changes that have been enacted.

These days, environmental controls are a top priority and you should stay up to date with them. It can be frustrating because each state has different controls and the modifications you'll need to make depend on the lane you've chosen. It's prudent to research the relevant state's environmental legislation and network with other truckers in your lane to figure out the impact of new rules.

Researching laws through online groups is also a great option since they contain a wealth of information. Just make sure you double check all the information on there since a lot of it is misinformed, or even worse, half informed. If you're scaling your business to the point where you'll hire other truckers, make sure you hire a full-time compliance employee who can make sure everything is in order.

Most owners do this job themselves but if it isn't to your taste, you should hire someone to do it. Whatever you do, do not neglect this function since the penalties can sink your business. When running a large operation, you'll have to stay up to date with financial disclosures as well. Strictly speaking, this isn't a trucking business requirement but it's worth noting. Hire an accountant or employ one who can track all of your receipts and prepare tax documents according to the latest IRS laws.

Remember that ignorance is not an option and the government takes a dim view of businesses that claim so. Always remain informed and spend some time each week subscribing to notifications of changes from the authorities. Consistent effort will ensure you remain compliant!

Conclusion

The trucking industry is fast-changing and there are multiple developments afoot that promise to change the landscape. The use of data in businesses has pushed managers to embrace machines more and the day of self-driving fleets isn't too far away. However, as I mentioned in the introduction, this day is still at least ten years away and you don't have to worry about it too much in the short term.

Scaling your business is one of the best ways to prevent it from becoming obsolete. Always focus on working with the best clients and relentlessly focus on increasing the quality of the clients you work with. Hire the best possible drivers and always pay attention to safety. In this business, safety trumps speed, so always prioritize that when hiring.

One of the best ways of knowing it's time to scale your business is when you're turning down work or are hauling loads that aren't as profitable for you. In such circumstances, it's best to hire another trucker and outsource the load to them. Scaling effectively means increasing the size of your fleet by one or two trucks every year. Don't make the mistake of going from one to 30 or more in a year since that growth is unsustainable.

Trucking tends to attract a certain personality type. Owner-operators are typically highly-independent people who don't want to be stifled by rigid regulations. This doesn't mean they flout safety rules. It's just that they prefer to do things their way. As you go along your owner-operator journey, you'll find many tips to smooth things out for yourself, outside of what I've given you in this book.

Remember that remaining compliant and safe are your top priorities. Without these two factors, your business is dead in the water. Never neglect them and always stay on top of them.

I'm positive that this comprehensive look at trucking has given you the confidence to set out on your journey to become an owner-operator. You don't have to become a large trucking company to be successful. There are many successful solo owner-operators so don't worry about it. Stick to what feels the most comfortable to you and always prioritize safety of yourself and others.

I wish you the best of luck in your journey! Please let me know what you think of the information that you've learned in this book and what you'd like to learn more about by leaving me a review.

Happy truckin'!

References

8 Reasons Trucking Companies Fail. (2020, April 12). Digital Dispatch. https://digitaldispatch.io/8-reasons-trucking-companies-fail/

Abbott, C. (2021, March 3). *New vs. used: There's much to consider when looking to purchase a truck*. TheTrucker.com. https://www.thetrucker.com/trucking-news/business/new-vs-used-theres-much-to-consider-when-looking-to-purchase-a-truck

Campbell, A. (2013, February 27). *Owner-Operator trucking challenges to success*. TruckingOffice. https://www.truckingoffice.com/blog/owner-operator-trucking-do-you-have-what-it-takes/

How to Find Trucking Contracts. (2021, July 28). Www.comcapfactoring.com. https://www.comcapfactoring.com/blog/how-to-find-trucking-contracts/

How To Start a Trucking Company | CDL. (2021, July 28). Www.cdl.com. https://www.cdl.com/trucking-resources/experienced-truck-drivers/how-to-start-trucking-company

Overton, T. (2017, March 9). *Step 6: Different types of trucking companies*. CDLLife. https://cdllife.com/2017/step-6-different-types-trucking-companies/

Ready for a Life Change? Becoming an owner-operator. (2019, May 23). Paper Transport, Inc. https://www.papertransport.com/things-to-consider-before-becoming-an-owner-operator-ready-for-a-life-change/

Transportation, L. S. (2019, February 7). *owner-operator vs. Company Driver - What's Your Best Option?* https://lonestar-llc.com/owner-operator-vs-company-driver-best-option/

Made in the USA
Middletown, DE
28 December 2022